SUM OF A GIRL

A MEMOIR OF SEX & SUICIDE

AMY SPOTO

Rip Van Winkle
P R E S S

Hudson, NY 12534

The names of certain individuals and
establishments have been changed.
Memories and dialogue have been reconstructed
to the best of the Author's recollection.

Copyright © 2023 by Amy Spoto

All rights reserved.

First trade paperback edition 2023

Edited by Laurie Chittenden and Brooks Becker
Cover art and layout by Vanessa Mendozzi

ISBN Paperback: 979-8-9881259-1-4
ISBN Ebook: 979-8-9881259-0-7

For my mother.

Walking together,
Barefoot on hot pavement in swimsuits,
You taught me,
To take risks,
Be adventurous,
Wild.
Free.

I love you.

"Let's see how far we make it!"

CONTENTS

Part One. Circa 2005–2016   1
    Fleeing   3
    The Last Supper   11
    You Won't Dance   25
    I'm Not a Slut, I'm an Alcoholic   39
    This Too Shall Hamburger   47
    Broken Gut   67

Part Two. Circa 1983–2004   77
    Misfit Kitten   81
    Quiet   85
    Joey | Joseph Stanley Kosnick III |
    Joseph Stanley Kosnick the Third Turd   89
    Pretty   95
    Saved by Sam   107
    Dirk   123
    Seven-Year Stretch   127

Part Three. Back to Circa 2016   157
    Broken Gut   159
    Truth or Die   181
    The House   195
    Add Water, Will Grow   207
    Trust Myself, Trust the Universe   219
    Undiagnosed   231
    A Love Letter   237
    The Road to Hell Is Paved with Good Intentions   243

    Afterword   245
    Thank You   250
    Get Help   251

PART ONE

Circa 2005–2016

"And in the end, we were all just
Humans drunk on the idea that love,
Only love, could heal our brokenness."

F. SCOTT FITZGERALD

Fleeing

It was the first of February and the only thing I knew was that I had to leave Fort Lauderdale. I flipped a coin. "If it's tails, I'll move back to New York. Heads, maybe Alaska."

Less than a week later, I packed my black 1998 Jeep Grand Cherokee with all my belongings: a small corner table from Target, books, a JanSport backpack stuffed with clothes, and Bunny—a once white, now oatmeal-colored stuffed rabbit, his left arm held on by a few stitches, his right ear tragically torn off by Sam, my ex-fiancé, during a fight. Bunny and I had been together since birth. At twenty-two years old, I still slept with him.

. . .

After driving twenty-four hours up the east coast, I arrived in Albany, New York.

My sister Jamie helped me unpack in her apartment as the freezing rain poured down and the man on the radio announced, "Today is the windiest day on record."

Fuck me. I left Florida for this, I thought.

When we were small, Jamie was called Gremlin and I was called Gremlin Two, the New Batch. We shared a room with bunk beds and counted sheep at night. Jamie's sheep always crashed into the imaginary fence and died. "Amy, I need to borrow a sheep," she'd request. I always said yes. When she got her own room, she let me sleep on a hard, wooden blanket chest at the end of her huge comfy queen-size bed. I gladly accepted. Jamie taught me how to drive a car and parallel park—once into an old man's car—and took me to my driving test. While she is three years older than me, people always asked if we were twins, followed by "Who's older?" We're both told we look like Pocahontas and the Land O'Lakes butter girl. Jamie had high honors and was the first to graduate high school and college in our family. She was the good one, I the bad.

IN ALBANY, JAMIE worked as an accountant for KPMG, one of the big four auditing firms. She dated her coworker, Dylan Murphy. I went with them to any after-work function that involved alcohol. We went to bars, bowling, and to a party at Dylan's apartment, which he shared with his brother Patrick Murphy.

Throughout the night Patrick shared pills with me, which I accepted without ever asking what they were. We did shots. We played beer pong in the basement. In the early hours of the morning, my eyes opened and my heart beat fast from alcohol and anxiety. Patrick was naked in the bed next to me. *Fuck, fuck, fuck,* I said in my head, because I thought I remembered passing out in bed alone. With pants on. The guilt was immediate. So too was the strong self-hatred. *Why do I get so drunk?*

That night became known as the "Houghtaling-Murphy, Houghtaling-Murphy hook-up," a joke everyone else laughed at. For Jamie and Dylan, there was no shame in what happened, in the joke, because they made their dating official and bought a house together soon after.

I, not knowing anyone else in Albany, moved into a three-bedroom apartment with Patrick and his friend.

Patrick and I played board games at Jamie and Dylan's house. We barbecued. We drank. The four of us hung out on my parents' boat. Standing on the dock, Jamie said, "You can't date him, it's weird." It was weird for me in a completely different way than what Jamie meant, and I knew we would never be dating. Even though sometimes I brought Patrick lunch, cleaned his room, and gave him a hand job when he wanted to hook up and I didn't. Even though he taught me how to navigate Albany and drew me cute little maps to get everywhere. First to Beff's, an Irish pub where I waitressed and finally made my own friends. Then to the Mohawk-Hudson Humane Society, where I adopted Broadus, a brindle and white pit bull who gave me a reason to get out of bed. To live. And finally, a map to Hudson Valley Community College, where I enrolled in the fall semester.

Before school started, I sat on the steps attached to our apartment, enjoying the midnight August air. The mix of whisky and feeling more like myself made me bold enough to politely ask Patrick to sleep in his own room, not mine. Patrick, not knowing we would never be dating, moved out the next day.

• • •

The September morning was sunny and crisp as I walked and wondered, "Am I the only asshole drunk on campus right now? Why did I pick three morning classes?" On a break, I sat outside the library writing a letter to my older cousin Chris. Chris and I were close when we were little, and I wanted to be there for him now.

In the letter, I told Chris that I had left Sam, left Pennsylvania, moved to Florida, then back to New York. That I was trying to get sober, and it wasn't working. As I wrote the words "I feel alone," I knew I'd never send it. Same as the other letters I wrote to Chris and never sent. I didn't want to bother him with my sadness because I knew it couldn't compare to what he must be going through in prison.

Standing, I packed my notebook back into my bag.

"Hey, aren't you in Schreck's class with me?" A boy I knew

to be named Nate asked.

"I am."

"He's the man, right?"

"He is!"

Schreck taught my only night class, Introduction to Chemical Dependency, from 6 p.m. to 9 p.m. Schreck was funny, kind, and talented as a teacher. After reading a paper I wrote on alternatives to AA, for people who didn't believe in a higher power, he made me feel like I could write well enough to be published. He himself had been published, which made his words more meaningful to me. Aside from teaching, Schreck was a judge for professional boxing and an all-around cool guy who talked about his love for his basset hound.

In that class, Nate normally spoke fast and often, sounding intelligent and never annoying. Like most who chose a major in substance abuse counseling, Nate also openly discussed being in recovery—all of us there to heal ourselves through the guise of helping others.

"So, how long have you been sober?" I asked Nate.

"Two years," he replied.

We talked for a few more hours, about school and life. When the sun set, I confessed, "My toes are numb!"

"You have flip flops on! We could've gone inside," Nate said, adding that his bus would be there soon.

"I can drive you home if you want," I offered.

• • •

At his house, Nate made pancakes for breakfast. Mine was in the shape of an elephant. Broadus got one in the shape of a bone. Nate bought me tickets to Bob Weir and RatDog at the Palace Theatre. We did homework together at his little square dining room table. He spoke passionately about science and unapologetically loved the Violent Femmes. He held my hand during an AA meeting and squeezed it three times. I. Love. You. The first time Nate disappeared, he admitted he was sober for two months, not two years.

• • •

At the Irish pub, I told my coworker and now friend what happened. That Nate disappeared. That he stole some money from me too. She said to leave. "It's only been a couple of months. You don't owe him anything and he's clearly still a crackhead. Plus he has a kid."

Days later, I thought of what she said as I sat with my forehead resting against the outside of a dirty bathroom door, pleading with Nate, "Please, can we go?"

An older-sounding woman answered from behind the bathroom door, "He'll be right out, hun." Emotionally tired from crying and waiting, I stood and walked to a room with red and gray plaid sheets covering the windows. A blue glow gleamed from a television, which sat adjacent to a black leather loveseat, cushions torn and cracked.

The floor held one bare, twin-size mattress with a man and woman passed out on it. A second twin-size mattress lay next to it, empty except for yellow stains. When the man who let me into the apartment sat down on the mattress, I asked, "Hey, got a cig?" Digging around in an ashtray from the floor, he handed me a half-smoked one, which I accepted with both reluctance and necessity. Defeated, I eventually dug them out on my own, one after the other.

When Nate came out of the bathroom, his eyes, normally wide, were sunken and sad. Empty. His mouth looked foreign. Slightly ajar and strange.

"I'm calling your brother," I said.

"No, she won't," Nate said to the others in the room. Then he added, "He won't come anyway," knowing his family was past the point of coming to help him. The people on mattresses did not know this, and Nate was told to get out.

· · ·

Trying to be better, I left the Irish pub and started working at the Golden Fox, a brand-new upscale restaurant. I told Jamie, "I can get you guys a reservation for New Year's Eve! Come see me in my fancy tie!"

I didn't know how to tie a tie, but the sweet sommelier did it for me. He was in his forties, fun, gay, and knowledgeable. He taught me how to open wine at the table, turning the bottle just so, wiping it with the cloth napkin, catching any remnants that ran down the side, properly pouring a taste for each guest, first the women, then men, in clockwise fashion. He made me feel smart enough to be working there.

Shortly after my shift ended, after I had served Jamie and Dylan their New Year's Eve feast, I sat drinking Jack Daniel's, reassuring the bartender, "Yeah, Nate will be here soon, he has my Jeep." When it was time to lock up and leave, it was clear to both of us, Nate wasn't coming.

"C'mon, I'll bring you home," the bartender said, adding, "Mind if we stop at a bar quick? My buddy's band is playin'."

Too sober and sad to dance, I nudged my way between intoxicated people to a blue velvet couch that sat at the far end of the bar. I drank there, watching women dressed in sexy, sparkly garb till the band played their last song and a man screamed, "Last call!"

Back in the bartender's dark, cold car, he tried to kiss me. Pushing him away, I said, "I'm really sorry, I just want to go home."

Angrily and aggressively, he told me to leave.

Compared to my own, Nate's apartment was closer to where I was by miles. Numb from the night, I walked. Nate's kitchen window was unlocked but blocked by a single tall white plastic shelving unit, which fell as I wrestled my way through. Turning on the light, Nate's roommate looked at me, rolled his eyes, and went back to bed.

"I need to go home. To Broadus," was all I could say when Nate finally came in.

"I'm so sorry, pretty head. Let me come with you. Please."

The ride to my house was silent. In my room, Nate and I stripped down. We climbed under the weight of my down comforter. We held each other tightly. We both knew what we wanted to do. Die.

"We could do it tonight, together," Nate said, his tears running onto me.

I agreed.

We put on the same clothes we had taken off and left, hand in hand, in the early hours of the New Year. We walked past dirty snowbanks littered with confetti, paper hats, and noisemakers. Inside the Jeep, we could see our breath. The cold torn leather seats stung the open skin on my lower back, where my sweatshirt met my jeans. I drove us to the apartment building I had so recently begged Nate to leave. He told me not to come inside this time, sparing me from the mattress people. As I watched Nate disappear into the lobby, I remembered what he said, "People always jump off this building but it's not high enough so sometimes they don't die."

Chain smoking, I watched couples holding hands and small groups of people, smiling and laughing. I imagined them on their way to breakfast. Clinking mimosas in celebration of hope. A fresh start. Something offered only by the New Year.

The sound of my phone brought me back to reality. "Why is Jamie calling me so early?" I wondered, thinking about how I wanted her to stay a normal person. The kind who went to brunch on New Year's Day. Not the kind who cried every January 1, the anniversary of her sister's suicide.

The thought of robbing her and my parents of their happiness with my own selfishness was hard and heavy but it was outweighed by how tired I was. I couldn't continue living solely for them. I had tried. For so long, I tried. Now it felt selfish of them to want me to stay. They didn't endure the daily life I lived. I wished they'd find peace after me, but I knew it wasn't something I'd ever have.

I couldn't answer the phone.

Back in my room, Nate and I sat on my bed, drinking boxed red wine. Nate showed me the pills he had just bought; he distributed them in an orderly fashion, instructing me which ones to eat first. The combination made us lighter. We talked more and faster. Not happy or sad but medicated.

"We should move to Florida. We owe it to your daughter. To my sister. To Broadus," I said.

"I'll go. I'll do anything with you," Nate said.

I packed the same things I brought less than a year earlier: some clothes, the table and books—but this time I had Broadus. I carefully packed his green bowl, with a big white bone painted on the inside, for his food. His red bowl, with white dog prints running along the outside, for his water.

We sobered up.

What we had done set in.

Nate called his mother, "I am doing this for HER, Mom. I can't be a dad to her there. I will see her. I'll get better and see her."

I called Jamie, "What the fuck do you mean you're in Georgia? You just waited on us at the restaurant! What about all your stuff?" she yelled, mad that I had left the camera she got me for Christmas, the couch she gave me, all of it.

She didn't know I left instead of died, for her. For my parents.

"Sorry," was all I knew how to say.

The Last Supper

January 2, the day after our plan to overdose failed, Nate, Broadus, and I arrived in Fort Lauderdale. The sun was still up, but it was dusk by the time I messaged my closest female friend in Florida, Jen. Jen understood first-hand what it felt like to fail at dying. She told me to come over to her parents' house, where she now lived.

Once there, Nate and I hung out with Jen and her mom before being brought to the guest room, which once belonged to Jen's older brother. In the morning, Jen's dad, a pastor, decided he wasn't comfortable with Nate and me sharing a bed. Instead of separating, we chose to go and be together, but Broadus stayed behind because we all knew Nate and I could be homeless, but Bro could not.

After Jen's, my days were spent filling out applications for waitressing jobs.

Name: *Amy Houghtaling*

Address: *Parked out front? Sunrise Blvd?*

At night, Nate and I alternated between windows open—welcoming the ocean breeze, eaten by bugs—and windows closed—bug free but sweating. Eating from the dollar menu, we hung out in bars till they closed, discussing life. "I don't know why I am the way I am. I don't know why I don't care about money. I don't want to go to college to get a job that I don't care about, to buy things. I don't care about things. I only care about love," I said.

He said that made me a good person.

That I was different.

"See, this is why I love you," he said.

"I don't know why I'm like that though. Why I'm me. Why I get sad instead of mad. Why I drink. That's why I don't judge anyone else."

"You drink because you're sad, and that makes you sadder," he said.

"Yeah, but I don't know how it started, chicken or egg."

I didn't trust my memory and could never decipher the order of things. Did I drink because I was sad, or was I sad because I drank? Was I weird before the drugs, or did they do that? Did my dad hit me because I was bad or was I bad because he hit me? All I knew was that there were parts of me I didn't understand, so other people must have that too. "I doubt the person who raped a kid set out and decided they wanted to be a rapist. Like, I bet they fought it. At least at first. Till they couldn't anymore. Same as you, with drugs. Me, with drinking. Some people are just stronger than others and beat it, I guess," I said, one hand clutching my whisky and the other on his thigh.

"I love that you're always touching me," he said.

In the small, dark bathroom, he boosted me on the sink, pulled his pants down, and pushed my skirt up.

• • •

A week later, still sleeping in the Jeep, Nate shook me awake.

"What are you doing? Who's that?" I asked.

"Get in the front, you drive," Nate said.

"Where are we going?"

"I told him we'd give him a ride to his hotel, he's cool," Nate said.

Driving down A1A, we were all quiet. I avoided the man's eye contact in the rearview mirror, but his stare was loud. Long, silent moments passed in the parking lot when we arrived.

"Go inside," Nate said.

"Why would I go inside? I'm not going inside," I said.

"What the fuck, man, I thought you said she was down," the stranger yelled.

"Dude, get out. Get out," I said, my voice never raised.

It's the addiction. Not Nate, I thought. Sober Nate wouldn't try to trade me for drugs. We loved each other. It was all we had.

• • •

Soon after, Nate started cooking at the Parrot Lounge and I went back to waitressing at Primanti Brothers. It started to feel hopeful. To be in love. To spend our days at the beach and nights working in restaurants. Happy.

When I worked five doubles in five days, I had enough money to sign a one-year lease for a studio apartment in what was once a 1970s-style motel. Concrete, L-shaped, the inground pool filled with dirt, dreams of what could have been buried, dead. It was here that Nate and I stood as our neighbor introduced herself to us.

"Hi. I'm Amie. We live right there. Come over tonight for a steak dinner in our tiki lounge," she said, barely pausing between words. Amie appeared to be in her late forties. Her hair was thin and dyed black, secured in a ponytail with a neon-pink scrunchie. She was shorter than me and wore men's nylon basketball shorts that went to her ankles. Her white breasts overflowed out of her tank top, and because she cut the bottom off, her portly white belly hung out too. With a manic look in her eyes and fast-paced speech, she explained that she and her boyfriend Reggie created an oasis on the small patio behind their one-bedroom apartment, located on the opposite side of the L as us, but still only three doors down. The invitation for real food was enticing. The desperation to believe it would all be okay, stronger.

"Nate, c'mon out back with me, man. I'll show you the bar I built," Reggie said.

Amie insisted I accept a tour inside. Dividing us.

Their bedroom was decorated in fabrics of deep dark plum. A large painting of a wolf howling in front of a purple moon hung above their pine dresser, where four lines of cocaine were neatly and evenly splayed.

"Oh, no thanks. We actually moved here to get away from that. Starting over, ya know. Please don't give any to Nate,"

She agreed she wouldn't, but I knew that wasn't going to be true.

THE NEXT MORNING, I woke up excited to get Broadus back from Jen and go for a run.

Back from both, I found Nate talking to our eighty-two-year-old neighbor and property manager, Bob. Bob had me wait in the courtyard while he retrieved a bag of treats from his apartment. As he fed Broadus way too many, he explained he had always had standard poodles and that he loved to show them off around town, in his convertible.

Bob asked how we were making out and if we used the mattress that the previous tenant left behind.

"Yeah, no other option, really," I laughed and added that it seemed new.

"Ah. Wait here," he said, handing me the now empty bag of Pup-Peroni.

Dragging over a white plastic lounge chair, Bob said, "It's better than the floor, don't be embarrassed."

"What do you mean," I asked.

"Go get another one. Just lay them flat, side-by-side. Make a box spring out of 'em."

To create illusions of rooms in the studio apartment, a white cinder block barrier went from the floor to a foot from the ceiling, separating the soft sage-colored living room from the blue bedroom. At the flea market the first thing I purchased was an old piano even though the only song I slightly knew how to play was Twinkle Twinkle Little Star. Loving classical music, I longed to learn it and keep some semblance of dreaming alive, imagining lessons in the morning before an afternoon walk with Bro. But my dreams quickly perished when the Parrot Lounge paid Nate for his first two weeks of work and he smoked it all away.

Without his own money, months went by where he stole my tips and my debit card too.

I blamed myself.

I should have hidden them better.

I would have hidden them better if I didn't drink.

Bank statements arrived, showing Nate used my card at known gay bars. He swore he only went there so guys would buy him drinks. He swore too that the bubble-gum pink, torn-apart dildo I found buried in the closet was there because he was high. That before me, he only let a guy suck his dick because he needed drugs.

Knowing Nate's next-door neighbor, an older man, had molested Nate as a kid, I breached the subject cautiously. "It's okay if you're gay, or bi. Maybe if you admit those things it will help you."

"I'm not, it's not that. I only love you, pretty head."

. . .

My twelve-hour shift ended at 10 p.m.

By quarter after, I was on my street.

The sirens were silent but the red and blue lights twirling created a pit in my stomach. "He's dead," I thought.

Our clothes were scattered in the courtyard, surrounding Nate, who was lying on his stomach, hands handcuffed behind him, screaming, smashing his head on the pavement as blood ran down his face. The officer tried to block Nate's forehead from the cement with his hand as I softly begged, "Stop, baby. It's okay, I'm here. It's okay. You're hurting yourself, baby."

The ambulance took Nate away, and then the police were

gone too. I stayed outside gathering our things from the yard. Inside I placed most of the pieces back where they belonged before discovering my laptop was missing.

Three doors down I banged and banged until Reggie opened the door, only a sliver of his face showing,

"Give me my laptop."

"Nate owed me money. Take it up with him," he said, shutting the door.

I banged more until he opened it again.

"Get the fuck in here and shut the fuck up," he yelled, pulling me inside, reaching his arm just above my head to slam the door shut behind me. Amie walked out from the bedroom.

"What the hell," she said, shoveling a forkful of food from a plastic Tupperware container into her mouth.

"I just want my laptop back."

"Who the fuck you think you are, comin' to my door like that?" Reggie yelled, his gun pointed at my head.

"I just want my computer back."

"You either dumb or brave, bitch."

The laptop was my only communication with my dad. The only thing I had outside of Nate and Florida.

Somehow, I left with it.

Retreating under the covers, Bro licked my tears and mirrored my sadness, always in tune with me. I told him I was sorry. I promised to get him out of this situation because he saved my life by giving me purpose: feeding him, walking him, loving him. His survival and happiness were my sole motivation for making it through each day.

. . .

A few weeks later, I met my boss, Todd, at Our Place, a small restaurant connected to a beachy hotel on Ocean Boulevard, not far from my apartment. We sat on stools at the outside bar. Behind us people jumped in a pool and laughed with their friends. It was typical Fort Lauderdale weather, sunny and super hot. I ordered a salad. Todd got bread and butter because they didn't have steak, basically the only thing he ate. One after the other, Nate's text messages came.

"When are you coming home?"

"Amy, come home."

"You say one beer and it always turns into hours later."

"Where the fuck are you? Come home."

He wasn't wrong. I did always stay longer than intended. The last to leave the party, the bar.

"I feel bad, I should go home," I said to Todd.

"Stay, it's fine."

"I did say only a couple though."

"You should do what makes you happy too."

"It's not that easy," I said before we switched to lighter subjects, which felt beyond good. To laugh. To be away from it all. Especially Nate, who that morning had begged me to leave him alone in the apartment so he could finish getting high from the crack he bought the night before.

The next message from Nate read, "You made me move here, I have no one and you have your friends. When I kill myself it will be your fault. You're doing this to me right now. YOU ARE KILLING ME."

Todd and I stopped laughing but still we ordered another round of drinks.

"I came home the other night and Nate was in the bathtub with an empty bottle of paint thinner. He drank it. He had a knife next to him and cuts on his arm. Before that he tried to hang himself in the closet with a scarf. My mom bought me that scarf for Christmas," I told Todd. I didn't mention that the ceiling broke from the weight of Nate, revealing his stash: steel wool, a lighter, an empty pipe, the destroyed pink dildo.

"What if he actually does kill himself?" I asked out loud,

although it was a question for myself.
It would be my fault.
It sank in.
It would be my fault.
"I'm afraid to go home. To find his body," I admitted to Todd.
"C'mon, I'll follow you."
The chain link lock allowed me a teasing glimpse inside, where I couldn't see or hear Nate. Begging him to answer me, I positioned one leg on the old hotel wall as leverage and pulled as hard as I could, surprised that it wouldn't break. Todd ran to the back door, but Nate pushed past him and ran down the street. Immediately I knew he was still high, and somehow that was my fault too.

Not knowing what to do, I went to bed and stayed there for days, only leaving to walk Bro. At night I drank the hours away. On the third day of missed work, I woke up to banging on my door. Todd's voice cracked, "Come outside, please Amy." We leaned against his old truck, the metal hot from the heat. "I have to fire you. You didn't call or anything."

"I know, I'm sorry. Don't feel bad," I said.

"I want to help you, but I don't know how," Todd cried, because we were on the same plane. He felt for me what I felt for Nate. Understanding this didn't make me know how to fix it.

The next day, Nate took the bus back to New York. To be with his family. To get sober. To take the heaviest burden off me, the task of keeping us alive.

Nate's leaving didn't feel better. It was just bad in a different way, which was why when my two friends, a brother and sister, came to check on me, I gladly accepted their invitation to the bar.

The sister went home first. Soon after, the brother and I were kicked out for breaking the strict *no girls in the men's bathroom doing lines* rule.

At his house, he took frozen vegetables from his freezer and mixed them into macaroni and cheese; I wondered how I had never thought of that. Bowls in hand, he led me to the roof. We ate there, watching the night sky before retreating to his room. He was gentle and sweet and when he was done making love, he fell asleep holding me. I admired his perfectly tanned skin, his high cheekbones, his long, dark hair. He looked peaceful. Removing his arm, which rested across my chest, I snuck out before the sun came up, because I knew that even on a good day, cocaine comedowns made me want to kill myself.

Back home, without Nate there, I felt truly alone.

I curled in bed, crying deep and heavy, hoping sleep could save me from the fact that I was unable to imagine a future where I wouldn't feel that way every day.

Knocking woke me.

Panic shot through me.

"I can't talk to anyone right now," I thought, but said nothing.

"Hello, Amy Houghtaling? This is Officer Bowling."

"Hi," I said, opening the door.

"Amy Houghtaling?"

"Yes."

"We received a call for a welfare check from Nathan. Are you okay here?"

"Yes," I said as they looked at me funny and walked away anyway. Leaving. Leaving, even though we both knew what I looked like. Not okay. Fucking terrible. And I wished I said that, or they did, but none of us said anything.

Less than a week later, Nate took the bus back to Florida to be with me. I got so many more jobs at so many more restaurants, cool ones that I loved on the beach at first, then shitty chain ones after, like Red Lobster.

"Hi, Ron, it's Amy. I'm really sorry I missed work without calling yesterday, my brother died," I lied because I didn't know how to say, "Oh, sorry I didn't call and couldn't come in, I just wanted to die instead." I didn't know how to explain that nothing mattered. Especially money. Nate had already stolen it all anyway, forcing me to put almost a year's worth of rent and everyday living on a credit card. Then he stole the credit card too, putting me so far in debt, ruining the perfect credit I had before him. What was the point in going to Red Lobster? What was the point in anything?

"Sorry about your brother, you can come back tomorrow, if you're ready."

"Okay, thank you," I said.

The next morning, I stood in the shower. The small blue-tiled bathroom resembled a steam-filled sauna. "Should I kill myself or go to work?" I asked Nate.

"Don't go to work," he replied.

My head rested on his soft chest, our naked bodies woven together in love and despair. The sound of his irregular heartbeat calmed me like it always had, allowing me to focus on synchronizing my breath to his. We made love, then planned our last day together. We took Broadus to the beach. We went to our last dinner and shared a grin only we understood when the parking lot attendant apologized, "I'm sorry, you have to pay the highest fee, you lost your parking ticket." We knew it didn't matter.

Back at the apartment, Nate left to get the deadly dose of heroin while I stayed behind. Sitting on a metal folding chair in the kitchen, I cried so hard it left no room for thought, my body focused on surviving, on inhaling and exhaling, violently. On having everything pour out of my face. Eventually though, even the energy for tears and snot ran out. So I smoked. Cigarette after cigarette, desperately drowning myself in Philadelphia whisky and the sound of Radiohead's *Kid A* album. *How many times has this song played?* I wondered as the effects of the whisky set in, allowing me the courage to text Jen.

"Hi. Can you stop by and let Broadus out tomorrow?"

I knew Jen would take care of Bro when I was not there to do so.

Next, I messaged Sam, my ex-fiancé. "I really did love you.

Goodbye."

The phone rang. It wasn't Sam to say goodbye or Nate telling me why he wasn't back yet, like I had anticipated.

It was my dad.

Over and over, he called.

The voicemail said, "Sam called me, I'm worried. Call me back, Ame," but same as my sister's calls, I couldn't answer.

There was nothing I could say, plus the letter was already written.

Then a ding sound, a text notification. Not Sam or Nate again, but my dad.

My dad had never sent a text message.

There were no spaces in between the words.

That one little detail. No spaces. I couldn't kill myself.

• • •

Knowing we wouldn't make it, separate or together, we left Florida and agreed it had to end when we got back to New York.

Broadus and I stayed with my parents on the days I worked at the Chatham Small Animal Hospital and with my sister and Dylan on the days I worked at Union College. Nate found a place with Matt McKane, a retired veteran he met at AA, who happened to live close to my sister.

Within a few weeks we went from only speaking on the phone to me pulling into Matt McKane's driveway. Nate stood on a bright-green, well-manicured lawn, baseball glove in hand, with a white T-shirt and jeans on. "I wore this because I know you think I look sexy in it," he said, smiling. We played a game of catch before going inside the small home, where the décor hadn't changed since the seventies and it smelled like canned vegetables. Nate's room was furnished with a wooden-framed twin-size bed and a matching wooden dresser with a small television on it. We borrowed a DVD, *Crash*, from the library and watched it in bed, drinking 40s because they were easier to dispose of than cans.

It was our attempt at abiding by Matt McKane's strict *no drugs in his home* rule, which included alcohol.

Nate swore drinking wasn't a trigger to smoking crack, which I wanted to believe because I wanted to drink. "It feels so good to be with you again," he said as we curled into each other, our skin familiar.

"Maybe it can be different now, better," Nate said before we made love.

I woke up before the sun. Nate was gone, so too were my money, cigarettes, and keys to the Jeep. I hated myself for drinking. Hated myself more for drinking with him. For putting myself in the position to miss work, because of him. When Nate called me a few days later it was to tell me that an ambulance had brought him to the psychiatric ward at Albany Medical Center. He hated himself too.

I visited him there once, but the barred windows and people were too much. When he was released, he went to Boston to get clean with a connection he had made somewhere along the line.

. . .

I found peace in my parents, in being with them when I wanted to be alone but didn't want to be alone. There was comfort in their routine, which hadn't changed much since I moved out during high school. Summer Friday was my favorite. On the boat, my mom made sausage, peppers, and onions. It wasn't the food that I loved. It was meeting her before anyone else arrived, drinking white wine, reading books on the back deck of the boat. Kayaking, discovering Murder's Cove. Throwing rocks in the river for Broadus, who put his whole head underwater to retrieve them. Laughing at Tugboat, my parents' Mastiff Lab mix who barked at every sailboat and at country music. It was watching my dad pull up around 6:30, walking down the dock, duffle bag in hand. It was the three of us.

Boat season over, every Saturday night my mom called Spring Garden and ordered beef and broccoli for herself and triple schezwan delight, extra spicy, for my dad, who always took out some shrimp to share with her. My dad picked a movie and my mom fell asleep on the couch from too much wine while he and I watched.

We didn't talk about my mom cleaning out the Albany apartment after I abandoned everything on New Year's Eve. Never about Florida, Nate, or the text message from my dad—nothing that led up to those events. We ate our food and watched our movie together.

That was enough.

You Won't Dance

When I found a full-time job, I stopped working at Union College with Jamie and started staying solely at my parents' house. In my small hometown, I ran into Ben, who said I should give him a call.

Ben had always felt safe to me.

I remembered that when I was fifteen and Ben and his friends were in their twenties, I passed out on Ben's best friend's couch. I woke up to Ben yelling at a guy who tried to do stuff to me while I slept. Ben brought me to a bedroom, where he told me to lock the door. He never tried anything himself. Later, at other parties too, I gravitated toward him.

I didn't end up calling Ben, but randomly saw him out again. At a gas station, he said I seemed sad and that I should come out of town with him.

Ben brought me on road trips to Utica, where we laughed and listened to Slightly Stoopid and Dispatch. We fished in the Hudson River and out west toward Oswego County, where we stayed in small cabins with bunk beds and caught salmon before the sun came up. We finished our evenings with Jack Daniel's, and nothing bad ever happened.

Ben gave me normalcy. Reprieve.

Without much thought, and after only dating a few weeks, Ben left the detached building behind his parents' house, and I left my parents' house too. We settled into a second-floor walk-up on Warren. We both worked during the day, which was a nice change from the nightlife of restaurants. I was home by 4 and done with my daily exercise routine, P90, by 5. When it was nice, we played wiffle ball in the empty lot across the street and after the sun set, we'd sit on the cement steps that led to the entrance of our building, drinking with our neighbors.

Feeling more level from exercise and life, I began to understand: if I wasn't going to kill myself, I needed to make more plans, beyond where I'd live and who I'd date, so I signed up for the next semester at Columbia-Greene Community College. I told Ben I'd have to quit my full-time job to waitress again, and he, being supportive and sweet, said he'd talk to his friend Alexander—the owner of 168.

Alexander didn't make me fill out an application, he only asked what my previous serving experience was and what animal I would be; a question, he said, that was on the actual paper application. I imagined Alexander wanted the type of person who provided something super clever in response to that. I was hired even though I didn't choose any animal at all.

After only a few shifts, I told Ben, "I think I might quit 168."

"What! Why?" he asked.

Internally, I thought of ingredients I'd never heard of. Cheeses I didn't know how to pronounce, taught to me by Elle, who had a timeless, classic beauty—Audrey Hepburn meets Twiggy. Elle never made me feel bad for not knowing things. She was nice and super funny, but I made myself feel bad because Elle was moving to California and my first feeling about that was relief, which was instantly replaced with guilt. I liked her. I didn't want to be that type of girl, but I didn't feel as good as her. Or as good as the tall, brunette bartender with bohemian styled jewels on her fingers, around her neck, and dangling from her ears. She spoke Swedish, as did Alexander, and the Head Chef too.

They were all smarter than me.

Happier too.

When the door leading from the server station swung open to the kitchen, the guys behind the line yelled, "Dance!" Everyone

always did. They moved their arms and bodies playfully.
Besides me.
I did not dance.
I carried a bag of red wine in my backpack. The wine was taken out of a box so it'd fit there. I ate ham and cheese hot pockets.
I wasn't like them.
"I don't know, I guess I'll keep going," I told Ben, who knew what I meant.
"You're just as good as them, ya know."
But I wasn't, and Ben discovered that too when I told him I had to go to Boston to see Nate, who had been sober long enough to reach back out and tell me so. Ben said he understood. That I had to go. I reassured him that maybe it meant nothing. Maybe Nate and I would only want to be friends. But I worried that if I didn't go, I wouldn't be able to live with the regret of never knowing what sober Nate and I could be; I worried I'd miss the opportunity to make Albany and Florida, the suicide attempts and addiction, mean something. If the pain of those experiences was the path to love, then it wasn't for nothing.

· · ·

Nate showed me around Boston. We saw *Juno* in the theater, and after, stopped to buy the soundtrack. We made love in his small room and before I left he promised to be better this time. On my second visit, he invited me for a sober party with his AA friends. People sat in different rooms. Someone played a guitar. I felt awkward, not knowing what to do with my hand, without a cup or bottle glued to it. Not knowing how to socialize without alcohol made me acutely aware, I didn't belong in their world.
Eventually, over the phone, Nate admitted his sponsor said so too. He couldn't be with me. He could be with someone sober though. Someone he met at a meeting.
"I'm so sorry, pretty head. I didn't mean for any of this. I

didn't mean to hurt you."

"Ashley?" I asked, immediately knowing it was the thin girl with long, shiny black hair from the sober party, the one who stood out with a wildness about her. She would have been my pick too.

"I swear it wasn't going on while you were here. We were just friends at first," he said.

My heart had a hard time comprehending that after everything, I was not the one who would be with Nate now that he was clean. I silently mourned for the future we never had, while still living with Ben, who without me asking for it, forgave me for my trips to Boston.

Ben and I tried to be what we were before, but I lacked the capacity to be nicer to him while he recovered from how I hurt him. I just wanted us to end. Or everything to end. But I didn't know how to say anything, so I kept my mind and body busy with motion. School. Walking. Working. Drinking.

• • •

Instead of coming home after 168, like I once had, I now stayed well past the one free shift drink. The other staff stayed for some, but by midnight it was always only the Head Chef and me left, sitting closely on black leather backless bar stools in the dimly lit restaurant, our conversations flowing over tumblers of whisky. When the bottle was empty, we walked the city streets with Broadus and his dog, Bernie. As the warm summer breezes turned cool, then bitter cold as winter set in, the Head Chef and I fell in love in a different way than I had known.

But because I am me, on the forest-green leather couch in 168, the Head Chef and I took it further than a loving friendship. Afraid of how sex would change our relationship, my mind blamed alcohol for the encounter, and I fixed it the only way I knew how—by breaking up with Ben.

Moving into my own apartment, I swore to myself that by living alone, without a boy, I would fix myself. Fix my drinking.

For reasons I never asked, the Head Chef never mentioned the night on the sofa either. Instead, we continued like we always had, walking the dogs, working, drinking. We snuggled too, sometimes in his Scandinavian bed, dressed in a white cottony comforter and pillows. It was cleaner, calmer, more comfortable than most men's rooms. Warmer.

The second time we had sex was there, only now his room felt cold and unfamiliar as he turned on his side, back toward me and said nothing after.

Dog walks during the day continued along railroad tracks and through alleyways, but at night I no longer stayed late with the Head Chef. Instead, I drove to Joe's. Joe's had buckets on the bar, catching water that dripped from the ceiling. It was the only bar in Stottville, full of regulars including my Aunt Maryann, Aunt Lia, and my cousin Jax. Besides my family, I enjoyed the company of the bartender, who had deep conversations about literature and music with me. I got to know the cook, who came out from the kitchen to stand on the makeshift stage, built behind where plastic bins held fifty cent wings on Thursdays, to sing. He sounded like Eddie Vedder as he sang Pearl Jam covers. Done with his set, he'd bring me into the bathrooms, where we sniffed lines until it was time to leave.

I drove the cook through a blizzard toward his parents' house.

"Pull over, pull in there," he said.

A radio tower stood tall.

"Let's climb it," he said.

"Go first," he told me.

Looking up to find the next cold metal bar to place my freezing, gloveless hands on, snow collected on my eyelashes. They were wet and heavy as I watched my phone fall from my hoodie, sinking into a pile of snow far below me. Disappearing.

I thought, "If I fall, this guy will leave me here."

We watched *Pineapple Express* on his parents' couch before he led me upstairs, where he laid blankets on a tan carpet in a small room furnished with an oak desk and an outdated computer. We stayed there for days. With no phone, I contacted no one until I returned to my apartment and opened my laptop to a Facebook message from the Head Chef:

"I don't know what to say. I'm just lonely and have nobody and soon I don't have my dog. And it feels like everything is going bad and I don't know what to do. Every time I do my best to be happy, everything is just bad. And I don't want to be everybody's number two. But fuck everything. I'm happy you are happy. I'm better off alone."

My fingers keeping pace with my mind, fervently I typed back:

"So, I don't even know where to begin... I guess you are number two to me, just like everyone else. Just like every other relationship I have ruined... number two because of drinking. The other night I stopped to get cig's and saw my cousin Jax who very easily convinced me to come have a beer at stupid Joe's... you know how that story ends for me, seven in the morning and I'm just going to bed. I am not happy by any means. You say I was hiding things from you, that I'm not telling you stuff...It's because I'm mad at myself. Mad I left you. Mad at how much I thought of you and wished I just stayed there with you. Mad at lying to myself and saying just one more drink then I'll go home and do my homework. I'm sorry that I did not call. That I was drunk and did stupid drugs and climbed a tower, maybe hoping to fall from the top, an accident no one would be mad at me for. I wish you were not sad, and I'm sorry I'm making it worse, by being a bad friend, for telling you my stupid problems. When I don't call it's because I'm embarrassed of what I'm doing. I love you a lot, you mean a lot to me, and I don't want the last couple weeks to mess up a friendship that meant and means the world to me. I miss you and you're not even gone yet. Sorry. Hugs. I am going to do something about my drinking. I'm hurting

myself, Broadus, school...everything."
Barely speaking to me in his last days, the Head Chef did not forgive me before he moved back to Sweden.

• • •

Needing respite, I went to Florida.
Standing under a palm tree in Todd's backyard, I was surprised that the cook from Joe's called me every day I was there. We hadn't hung out enough for that. "I guess it's nice," I thought.

• • •

When I returned to Hudson to resume classes at Columbia-Greene Community College, the cook signed up too, and somehow he began regularly spending the night at my house. I proofread his papers. He helped me with my poetry and made me dinner. We took Broadus and his pit bull on trails and camped on the river in Stuyvesant. I went on rescue missions with him to get his brother out of the crack house on the corner of Carol and Short Street. I held him when he cried about it, cried about his relationship with his dad, about his life.

I thought, *If I'm nice to him, if I show him love, he will be the person I know he is.* Not the other person I saw glimpses of. The one I was warned about. The one who made my friends and family say, "You can't come if he's with you." The one who tagged his stupid nickname on my wooden bedframe, made by my father; on a jewelry box I loved, given to me by my mother; on walls and bar tops at restaurants, everywhere. The one who was normal when I went to sleep but woke me up in the middle of the night, fumbling as he tied strings from tables to doorknobs, attempting to booby trap the house. Who videotaped me while I slept. Who yelled at me at Hagor's Harbor while mushing steak between his gums, "It's your fault I have no teeth! You made me get 'em fixed."

I didn't know what drugs he was doing. If it was crack, he didn't act like Nate.

When he was fired from Joe's and started to steal my money and debit cards, I told myself, "I will not do this again."

He was not Nate. He was not a good person with a drug problem. He was shit.

Begging him to leave didn't work, he was persistent in his pursuit to stay. Locking him out didn't work either; he broke in through windows, the kitchen then the living room.

"Well, ma'am, if you let him sleep here for consecutive days, he has a right to be here," the officer said.

"I never gave him a key. He's not on the lease. Nothing in this apartment is his, he doesn't live here," I said.

It didn't matter.

• • •

With the Head Chef gone, Alexander, the owner of 168, had Bernie. Now he and I went on dog walks every night after work, making him become my closest friend.

Because I hated smoking and walking, Alexander and I stopped at the gazebo that sat on the grass in front of the Columbia County Courthouse. Lying side by side, we passed a cigarette back and forth, talking. Sometimes about our histories. Our demons. Relationships too. "You always see the good in people. Oh...he can sing goooood. He's goooood at poetry." Alexander mocked me one night, making us laugh.

THE NEXT DAY, Alexander asked me to come keep him company while he prepped for the evening. In his pristine kitchen I scrubbed pots in the big bay sink while he worked behind the line.

"Zak likes you."

"No, he doesn't. He doesn't even talk to me."

"He does! He talks about it. Just go out with him, get away from Eddy Fucking Vedder."

ZAK WAS THE sous chef, he started one week before me. We worked together for almost two years at 168. Recently, in preparation for MMA fighting, he cut his dark-brown, emo-styled hair and took out his lip ring. His features stood out more because of it. His beard somehow seemed silkier. His eyes, which slightly changed color depending on his shirt, looked a brighter blue. His sexy symmetrical tattoos on his forearms contrasted more beautifully against his Sicilian skin tone.

Being too consumed with the Head Chef, with my past, and with present problems made me unable to fully comprehend what Zak was. A person who started my Jeep when it was cold out. Who cleared the snow from it too. Who, during staff meal, took the chicken off the bone for me because I was weirded out by meat. Who was only three years younger than me but felt galaxies apart because of our life experiences. A kind innocence remained in him, not me.

"I'm taking the boat out to go wakeboarding tomorrow, wanna come?" I asked Zak.

Zak got in the backseat, wearing a long sleeve water shirt that was tightly plastered to his body. Luke, Alexander's older brother, immediately made fun of him for it. Zak took it like a champ. He always did. Through all the pranks and teasing, he knew the 168 crew bullied him like a big brother, in a loving way, not a mean one.

Standing back in the kitchen with Alexander, I said, "I told you Zak doesn't like me, he didn't even talk on the boat!"

. . .

I SAT ON the back porch of 168, surrounded by cardboard boxes that had been broken down. The smell from the dumpster in the alley was intensified by the heat. I looked at my bandaged hand, which earlier that morning was slammed in a heavy steel door as I tried to escape my apartment. Zak saw it and immediately knew who did it.

The next day, Zak asked me to sit with him in the passenger side of his black 1999 ½ Jetta, so he could play a song he wrote.

"You don't dance, but I'm not asking
You aren't dead, but your eyes are lying
So sad.

I'll be on the rooftop singing you a lullaby
You'll be on the high rise down by the riverside
Take the boat out on a rainy day
So set your sails away, keep the demons at bay

This is a song for the evergreen forest on the night you screamed
Awake from slamming doors that don't exist on tattered digits and broken fists
Why do you settle for this?

You collapse, from the pain inside
You don't dance and now I know why
Please just breathe you are vacant to me

I'll be writing poetry about this fuckin tragedy
And you should realize what it is that I've kept inside
But you're so naïve to this game
So set your sails away, keep the demons at bay
You don't dance, but I'm not asking."

● ● ●

"I'll pick you up after work," I told Jamie.

"Just take it off!" she half seriously begged back.

"No way. Something bad always happens to me on New Year's Eve. I'll just come get you from the party. I'm not going inside."

At almost 11:30 p.m., I beeped and she came right out. "Wanna go watch the ball drop at Mom and Dad's?" she asked.

Normally we received a call from my dad at midnight. "HAPPY NEW YEAR..." That year we got to say it in person.

Back at my apartment, Jamie and I put on new Victoria Secret Boyfriend Sweatpants my mom had given us for Christmas. We opened red wine, played *Mario 3* on the original Nintendo, and went to bed before the bottle was gone.

My eyes opened, shocked awake from the pain of being dragged out of bed by my hair. I heard Jamie yelling but didn't know what she was saying. It felt fast, blurred. I wondered how two policemen were already standing in my living room while Eddy Vedder yelled, "I'm not a drug addict, she is," pointing at my sister who had never done drugs in her life.

Staring at the window, broken by him again, I spoke. "He has a warrant in Saratoga for not paying child support." This time, that was enough to make the police care. After he was arrested, he never showed back up to my apartment. Never called.

● ● ●

Zak walked me home. He opened car doors for me. He bought me a teapot, tea, and a house plant with deep-green leaves and red spiky flowers when I was sick. He was not a drug addict. He had a job. And teeth. In a joking but true way I told him, often, "You're too pretty for me!"

When he took me to his parents' pond, he drew a heart in the snow over the frozen water. I knew he was too good for me too. He and his family, nice and normal, I'd never be like them.

• • •

My father took me to a house. The front porch was made of broken, cracked concrete. A metal awning stretched over it, painted white with one lime-green line to match the dirty lime-green aluminum siding. The backyard was long and narrow with no trees. The windows were old, it was too dark to see inside. My dad explained he used his home equity line of credit to buy it. I could pay the mortgage and have it, if I wanted. Without ever seeing the inside, I agreed. Then invited Zak, who I had only semi-officially been dating for three months.

When I got the key, Zak, Alexander, and I went after work. The kitchen had fake bricks plastered to the walls, the cabinets were dark brown. The living room had a drop ceiling and coffee-colored paneled walls, making it feel smaller than it already was. Suffocating.

The bathroom had a long Pepto-Bismol pink counter with two sinks. There were three small bedrooms. Hardwood floors full of staples with tiny shears of rug remained, reminders that men in hazmat suits had ripped the wall-to-wall carpeting out. In the basement (where the only working light was), sipping champagne Alexander had brought as a surprise, we looked at the far wall where the foundation was cracked all the way across.

"Keep the glasses," he said.

A gift from 168.

• • •

Zak kept cooking at 168. I finally graduated with a degree in Human Services and left the restaurant world, hoping I could finally fix my drinking and move on with life.

Not far into my new career, I called the Domestic Violence

Shelter, where I was a counselor. "I'm so sorry I didn't call sooner. I had a family emergency," I said.

"I understand an emergency, Amy, but it's unacceptable that you didn't call before your start time," the director said.

A story fell so easily out of my mouth. A drunken uncle I rescued and got into rehab. "I had no time and no cell service," the tale concluded, leaving me feeling dirty and disgusting, like a relapse on every level of my being because after Florida I swore I would never miss work because of drinking. I would never be too sad to call in. I wouldn't tell lies to cover it all up later either. But survival mechanisms are there for a reason.

"I'm sorry you had to go through that," the director said, and I knew that in exchange for being a garbage human and a liar, I got to keep my job.

The next day I drove toward the bridge for my 11 to 7 shift, the mid-morning sun shining heavily on the Catskill mountains. *If I crashed my car it'd look like an accident. No one would be mad at me,* I thought. Emotional stabbings by my own inner voice; quick words that wounded me deep down. *Do normal people think like this on the way to work?* I wondered, and let the thought go to somewhere unknown inside of me because after Florida I finally accepted that I would never kill myself; I couldn't listen to that voice.

To me.

I'm Not a Slut, I'm an Alcoholic

Near the 4th of July, sheets of rain poured down. Listening to the sound, I sipped a crisp, cold glass of Vinho Verde, reading *Dry* by Augusten Burroughs. As the storm grew stronger, Zak lit the candles he had gathered in preparation for the power going out, then sat with me. We watched lightning brighten the dark sky, we heard bursts of thunder, followed by a sudden crashing and splashing beneath us.

Opening the hatch on the floor, we climbed down, stopping at the last stair not covered by water. Stray socks floated past us in a sea filled with stacks of cinder blocks and clumps of clay. Shining the flashlight, we saw the white vinyl siding of our neighbor's house.

They yelled over, "Hey, you guys okay?"

"Yeah, we're fine," Zak yelled back.

At the dining room table, I sipped my wine while trying to calm Zak down. "There's nothing we can do about it now, it's already happening."

"Amy, the fucking wall is falling down."

"I know but it's too late, we just have to wait and deal with it when it's done."

"Can you please just call your dad?" Zak said.

MY DAD HAS high cheekbones, his hair is long, to the middle of his back. He is nicknamed Chief and Ponytail. Ponytail, even though for over twenty years my mother has stood behind him, braiding his hair, securing it at the end with a tiny elastic tie.

My dad is also called Animal, by men who knew him from his past, when he partied. His tougher, crazier days. Before he quit drugs. He is physically strong. His arms, massive. In school, boys joked, "Your dad got his muscles from throwing engines around all day!" His character is strong too. He pulls strangers' cars out of ditches. He is generous, lending his tools and fixing cars and plowing driveways for little to no monetary profit. People pay him back with a bottle of Dewar's or, if they know a trade, with that, which was lucky for me in this situation.

"Nothing we can do right now. I'll have people over in the morning," my dad said.

In mud-covered boots, Aunt Lia's boyfriend worked the cement mixer under a man-made tent, built to block the rain from the storm, which had carried over from the night before. Other guys I knew, and some I didn't, helped too. Skilled men built the wall while Zak and I shoveled out buckets and barrels of heavy earth and dirt, trees, and plants.

Zak went back to work the next day, and the rest of the team dwindled down too. By day three or four, only my brother and I stood in a seven-foot trench together. The sun was hot, sweat dripped into my eyes as I looked up at Zak, dressed in a clean T-shirt and nice shorts.

"I'm going to Kirwin's to play Magic," he said.

"Oh, okay."

"Are you mad?" he asked.

"No, do what you want."

"It's just that it's my only day off and I told Corey I'd play."

"Okay, have fun then," I said.

In general, I wished Zak wanted to help me. That he cared about fixing the house. Or at the very least, today, knew not to leave me in a hole while he went to play a card game. But I refused to tell him what to do. Or ask him to stay.

Looking at my lockjaw, the dentist asked, "Are you stressed out?"

"No, I don't think so," I said.

"Nothing major is going on in your life?"

"No, not really."

"I ask because women tend to carry stress in their neck and jaw. Are you sure you aren't feeling extra stress?"

"I mean the wall to my house just caved in," I said, laughing and repeating, "But I don't think I'm stressed out."

I wasn't lying to the dentist.

Just unknowingly to myself.

• • •

Across the street from our house, Zak, Broadus, and I walked the yellow trail at the Greenport Conservation Area. "We need to have at least one day off together. We need quality time. Not just eating dinner together once a week," I said to Zak, who explained he knew but needed to hang out with his friends too. Understanding and agreeing didn't change how I felt in his absence though. I craved a deeper connection, desired day trips to random places to hike and have beers, car rides to nowhere. Adventures, with a soul mate to explore the planet with, to make life worth it.

Wondering if my needs were naïve, I was quiet for a few more steps before I said, "I want you to want to hang out with me. I feel like I have to beg you to do stuff with me. It's embarrassing. I feel stupid saying this right now."

"We need to find hobbies to do together," we both agreed. We threw out ideas. Backpacking overnight in the mountains. Painting or pottery classes. We tried nothing.

Like the foundation of the house, we saw the cracks but only made small attempts to stop the crumbling.

・・・

Twice, Zak camped with me on the river. A few times he went with me to a friend's house. His effort.

I tried one game of Magic: The Gathering. I lost a few rounds of streetfighter, but never attempted any of the other video games he played at night. "Please come to bed with me. Just one night. Or just lay down for a little while," I said, a few times a week as he pulled the bedroom door shut. I heard only his voice; the headphones blocked the noise of the guys he played PlayStation with. I never yelled or started fights about it, but did occasionally bring it up, always apologizing the next day because I couldn't remember the details, how the conversation got started, or what my exact words were. I swore I'd drink less. Not that he asked me to. My effort.

・・・

Different obsessions continued to gradually create a growing gap between us, and we were too nice and polite about it. I think it was out of love. For me, also admiration. I saw the beauty in Zak's consumption. He perfected any hobby he immersed himself in. In high school playing the guitar, being a chef when we met, and MMA after that. I drew him pictures and made him cards telling him how much I believed in him, how talented and amazing he was. How beautiful. I meant those things wholeheartedly. He made me cards too, poems written in hearts crafted out of construction paper.

"He's silly. He makes me laugh when I see him on my lunch break," I told Jamie, trying to convince myself, out loud, it was enough.

"Really, Amy," she said.

LATER, I JOURNALED.

"*I feel disconnected from everyone. If I listen to my inner voice, I feel lonely with Zak. I want more. That is unrealistic or selfish, or both, but I need something more. But I love Zak. I don't want to hurt him. I want us to change together. Grow together. He is beautiful and good. He is silly and I love that. We just need real time, but HOW?*

Goal: Create connection and meaning in my life."

• • •

Late summer, the air was still warm after sunset. I sat with my friend from high school, Whitney, drinking later than intended on a work night. Heather, Whitney's girlfriend, walked out to the backyard, where we were, and heard Whitney trying to count the number of people she had slept with.

"Oh my god, Whit, I've only had sex with five people before you!" Heather said.

"WHAT! Yeah right," I said.

"It's true," Heather said.

Trying to count mine, I half seriously asked, "Including girls?"

"Yes, idiot," Heather said.

"I can't remember the Radiohead guy's name in Illinois or the guy on Morris Street in Albany. That's so bad," I said before coming up with an estimated number, similar to Whitney's.

Whitney jokingly justified us to Heather, "It's like an average of three a year. Since we were fifteen. That's not a lot!" Fifteen was the age when Whitney and I were inseparable, but the relationship started the year before when we played modified basketball together. After practices, we'd walk to Whitney's house to make Ellio's pizza and listen to Mary J. Blige's *My Life*. When we made it to my house we hung out in my basement bedroom, where Whitney rolled blunts because I didn't know how. We did projects, like painting a giant Wu Tang sign on my wall because we were both better at being active than talking, which was what bonded us more than music and sports alone.

"My number should be lower. I've been in a serious relationship since I was fourteen! It should be, like, a total of six," I said, and added, "But, in my defense, every time I've cheated I was drunk. I'm not a slut, I'm an alcoholic."

"Oh my god, I love you!" Whitney said, laughing.

"It will be the name of my book: 'I'm Not a Slut, I'm an Alcoholic!'" I said, laughing too, being sure to never share the unfunny parts of stories, or what happened in the direct aftermath of my mistakes—like when I was kissed by men who were not Zak, at a wedding and at bars, I hid in bed hating myself, burying my secrets in my journal, promising to change, and scribbling rules.

"No Whisky.

Never do shots.

No liquor at all.

No more going to bars.

Only go to the bar with Zak.

Only drink at friends' houses,

Fix the drinking, fix myself."

In addition to the rules, I sentenced myself to solitude, declining invitations to hang out because I knew my only salvation was to stop drinking so nothing bad could happen. The level of loneliness that created was not sustainable though; my punishment faded and ended after a few days. Mostly because I was hungry.

Back at bars, I ate food with friends because that was fun, it's what I knew. With enough time and drinks, I'd air my faults with no filter, anecdotally, for amusement. "Those guys were probably mad I was still up! Talking, trying to swim...Like, 'Damn, this bitch is like a horse, she won't go down,'" I said about the time I was roofied in South Carolina while Zak sat alone on a porch smoking a joint, instead of coming out with Whitney and me, and it worked. People laughed.

They also laughed when Heather told her part of the story too. Me making my way back to the condo still drugged as she fed me pizza, lying on the couch sipping water sideways from a cup, saying, "I'm so good at Myrtle Beach!"

We added "I'm so good at" to an assortment of scenarios:

Black out on a Tuesday, "I'm so good at Tuesday."

Ate too much, "I'm so good at tacos."

Alexander and Heather became "so good" at CrossFit. Then "so strong" from it.

When Alexander killed himself, Heather tattooed an infinity sign on her shoulder. "So Strong" was scripted inside of it, lineage of me being hilariously roofied inked permanently on her body.

This Too Shall Hamburger

February 2.

A few days before Heather's dedicatory tattoo for Alexander. My friend Sean and his new girlfriend, Maggie, sat at the high top at 168, with Zak and me. The amuse bouche and white fish roe to start, Swedish meatballs, filet mignon, tacos, and a BLT with hummus followed. Bottles of petite Syrah and countless cocktails later, Alexander came out from the kitchen and stood near our table.

"Are you still not smoking?" I asked, because he was forever trying to quit.

"I smoked one cigarette last night because I was sad and cried," Alexander said as everyone at the table continued to talk.

When he walked away, past the doors labeled "water closet," past the empty coat rack, I said, several times, "Alex, come back," but he left through the front entrance anyway, only reappearing right before we left.

We could see our breath as we stood on the sidewalk talking.

"I think I'm going to be the manager at Bystro," Alexander said.

I'm sure we asked if he would sell 168. Or keep it and hire a new head chef. I can't remember his answer.

I know Alexander and I hugged goodbye. I'm almost positive we said, "Love you." But I'm not certain.

Before the car was put into drive, Zak sent Alexander a text message, "Don't think I didn't hear you say you were sad. I did, and I'm sorry."

Alexander responded, "This too shall hamburger."

Two days later.

February 4th.

Whitney opened the door to the small conference room my staff meeting was held in and said, "I need to talk to Amy."

We stood near the water cooler. There was no one else in the hallway.

"Alex shot himself," she said.

I didn't think, *He is dead*. I just thought, *He shot himself*. Jamie had a friend with an uncle who shot himself and lived.

To Whitney, I only said, over and over, "I need to go outside. I need to go outside." Then, "I need to smoke," even though I didn't smoke in the morning anymore, graduating to only at night, with drinks.

If Whitney said any more words, it was quick and I don't remember them; the facts were presented, and she was gone, back to her office downstairs. As much as we loved each other and had been friends since middle school, we didn't know how to hug and be there in that way.

Searching through my bag for cigarettes that were not there, I gave up. Fingers interlocked, resting on my head, I stood in the middle of three gray cubicle walls, crying.

"Amy, what's wrong?" my boss asked.

"I have to leave."

Even though Zak and I had impulsively eloped in January, Luke was the first person I called when I got into my truck.

Not yet out of the parking lot, I barely got out, "Are you okay?"

Low and monotone Luke responded, "Did Alexander hurt himself?"

"Yes," I said.

"I have to go," he said.

Alexander's own brother didn't know yet.

Fucking small towns.

"Hi," was all I said to Zak, who knew I knew by my voice.
"I just got off the phone with Eli. He told me."
Eli was Zak's best friend. They played in a band together right after high school. Eli basically lived at our house before he met a girl and followed her to Paris. Gossip of death traveled far and fast, especially this kind.
"I'm driving to the brewery," I said.
"Leaving in a minute, meet you there."
It was before 11 a.m.; the brewery wasn't open. When I arrived, the head brewer was outside. As I walked toward him he said, "Not you, I can't see you right now."
He and I hugged tightly, crying together. The owners, Sean and Lou, stood outside too. Standing on small stones, we took in the shock and pain together. The loss. We felt it for each other because for the last eight years Sean, Lou, and I had been bonded together because of Alexander, because of 168.
We started drinking, people filtered in and out all day and night, but none of it mattered.

• • •

The next day, Luke called and asked me to meet him at Bates and Anderson Funeral Home. He couldn't bring his girlfriend.
"I don't want her to see this," he said, which wasn't alarming to me.
I didn't think, *See what?*
Instead, my subconscious assumed this invitation would be the same as the rest, because I'd been to Bates and Anderson Funeral Home more times than I cared to count, since as young as I could remember. First, barely five, for my gramma Annie, where I sat in a folding chair in the front row, reserved for family, swinging my legs that didn't reach the floor. My black patent

leather shoe flew off my foot. Thud. Bounced off the casket, cutting the silence with laughter.

For Alexander, it started the same way. The usher held the door open. He looked at me with a sorrow in his eyes that said, "You again." I hung my jacket in the closet, like I always did, but unlike the other times there was no book to sign. No small plastic card with a prayer on the back to keep as a memento. There was no line of people waiting to go into the room to the right, to kneel in front of the coffin, hug the family, and move on, awkwardly making small talk while looking at poster boards full of pictures of the deceased, feeling validated if you made the cut. Proof you meant something.

For Alexander, there were five of us. We waited in the foyer near the white staircase, Lucas went in first. When he came out, he announced, "Yup, I checked, he's dead!" Like the Queen's Guard, the usher did not change his facial expression, he stayed still and stoic as we laughed.

Zak held my hand. We went in next. Where a rich wooden casket with plush silky insides normally sat, something else stood—a metal table, maybe. Alexander wasn't dressed in thoughtfully chosen clothing, no white chef coat or suit. Instead a sheet covered his body, I think. There were marks on his head, I was afraid to ask if they were from the gunshot wound, but I did.

"I'm sorry I let you come with me, I didn't know it was going to be like this," I said to Zak. Feeling the need to protect him because he was newer to death than I.

"I wanted to, for you. And for me," he told me, which I knew was true because Alexander and Zak had their own friendship—the unique kind that can only be born in a kitchen.

⋯

To honor Alexander and help his family, Zak and a fellow friend, the owner and chef of Nudel, prepared the dishes for the final weekend of 168.

"Can you go to Grazin and get my chef coat?" Zak asked me.

"Of course," I said and went out through the back kitchen door, walking onto the wooden porch that held the heart of my memories. It was there we would go to just be ourselves, to get away from customers and cooking. Where Bernie sat, Broadus too sometimes, both always good for a pat and a hug. Where Alexander and the head chef pranked Zak, recording it for YouTube. Where we sat and smoked near the sort of triangle-shaped rock, painted into a Swedish flag, discussing nothing and everything. Where I still snuck to, long after I left 168, stopping in the white minivan I drove for work, stealing a quick ten minutes with Alexander before heading off to a home visit.

Walking the five blocks through the alley I realized it was the first time since everything started that I was fully alone and semi sober. Dark and deep yet calm, I thought how I wished it were me Alexander had texted that morning. A water gun emoji. An almost hilarious last text, if it wasn't so fucked up. *Maybe I could have stopped him*, I thought, before wishing I went to Gaskins with him and Elle. A sunny Sunday afternoon, I was lying on the living room floor with Broadus. Zak and Eli were on the couch. All of us hungover. We said no and I wished I had said yes. I wished I said yes, too, when he called from the table of the tattoo shop. "Come get this tattoo with me," he said and sent a picture of a T Rex skeleton, 'Hamburger' written in bubble letters at its feet. I thought Hamburger was an inside joke with him and Elle, so I didn't go. I didn't want to overstep. I wished I did.

I thought of the Head Chef, how we fixed our friendship, and I wished Alexander and I had time to do that too. We were talking, but there was tension between us over something frustrating he said...Most of all I wished I'd been a better friend, at what I later learned was the end.

Guests were seated, tables turned over, happily I distracted myself running food until the restaurant was quiet and empty, besides Luke and me. Sitting with him, my soul knew, nothing would be the same again because the building that created a bond between me and three Swedish boys—him, the Head Chef, and Alexander—would be sold. Out of us, I would be the last left living in Hudson, a place that never felt like home until I met them.

Finally having enough alcohol, Luke and I climbed the stairs past the second-floor apartment, where Elle and the babies slept, and then we made our way to the third floor. Knowing the tenants weren't home, we opened the door and each chose a room. Alone in the dark, I fell into blankets and pillows that were fluffier and better than my own. Waking with a sense of panic in the early morning hours, I tiptoed through the apartment and searched for my phone. I wanted to call Zak. I wanted to go home so bad.

Unable to find it, I thought about waking Luke, but knew I couldn't, I wouldn't. Hoping fresh air would help, I sat outside on the cement steps. Leaning on the cold black metal railing that separated the apartment's entrance from the restaurant, I noticed how empty and still the streets were, life was. I reached into the sweatshirt I wore and pulled out a pack of crushed Marb Reds, not mine, not my brand either; I lit one anyway. Too thirsty, it made my head spin and I hated that I was smoking it, hated that I didn't go home with Zak, my husband, the night before.

Why would I do that? I wondered before telling myself I had to stay with Lucas. He was my best friend. His brother died. I had to be there for him. *But why didn't Zak stay with me?* I thought, feeling all alone waiting for the world to wake up.

• • •

The last Saturday.

The Head Chef arrived from Sweden, he had lost his childhood best friend, a brother. The grieving felt like day one again, but we did what needed to be done. Food went out again. The last customer was served. 168 was closed.

When morning came, I walked into our bathroom and asked Zak, "What happened?"

"You fell when we got home," he said, continuing to brush his teeth as I put the rod, shower curtain still connected, back up between the walls and washed off the night before, preparing for more.

Our small group of people met at Sean's house, chosen because it was walking distance to the cemetery. Together, we walked up the steep hill to lay Alexander's ashes down with his family and close friends. At his grave, prayers were replaced with words that originated from Neil DeGrasse Tyson, assuring us we were connected to Alexander through the stars.

· · ·

Alexander was ahead of his time with food: elk, wild boar, snake, and llama, served with sides of pepper foams and gels. But beyond the respect and desire for sustenance, people visited 168 for the experience that Alexander provided. The darkly lit atmosphere made you feel good in Alexander's company, in his restaurant, his home.

The magic when Alexander visited you though, that was really special. I know that besides my house, daily he walked and biked to Bonfiglio, MOD, Le Gamin, Hudson River Tattoo, and the 10 a.m. CrossFit class. In these places and beyond, he built bonds with his magnetic, witty, and hilarious charm and always offered up advice, even if you didn't want it. "You should do it this way!" he'd say.

When Alexander was moody, any annoyance quickly dissipated the second he smiled again. His cute, chubby face was boyish, young, and impossible to stay mad at. He was a good old soul and the whole city of Hudson loved him. For that, a memorial was planned on March 20th, two days after his birthday, so he could be celebrated.

Alexander's wife and Luke asked if I wanted to speak. In my journal I wrote,

"Maybe I should get over this public speaking thing.
Then there is the part of my brain that always feels like
WHAT IS THE POINT.
Who am I to speak and who cares what I say.
In the grand scheme of things,
NOTHING MATTERS.
NOTHING MATTERS.
Except love?
I know Alex loved me, he told me all the time. He also showed it. I think?
He painted my mailbox in the middle of the night. The first, my favorite, black with a goldfish in the middle. Then blue with yellow banners, the Swedish flag.
With the same yellow, he painted three faces in my driveway: a smiley one, a straight faced one and a sad one.
Randomly, for no reason at all, he bought me a shoehorn from Ikea.
He came over unannounced every week, on his way to Price Chopper. Hanging out in my yard, telling me how I should fix my house,
"Paint the walls, the guest room is an ugly color."
He was right.
He was always right when it came to projects.
I could tell the story of when my father dropped me off at the Chatham Brewery to meet friends. The cab driver who agreed to pick me up bailed. I posted on Facebook asking if anyone in the area could bring me home. Sara said she would but didn't. Instead she sent a crackhead, covered in blood, pulling a deer from the back of his truck, 'I hit it on the way here.' I declined to go with him. Zak said he was too tired to come, plus he had to work in the morning. True and fair. Alexander was the only

person I knew I could call. And without hesitation, late Saturday night, after he worked all day, he drove 20 minutes to come get me. Then 20 back with me.

I would leave out that Alex pulled into the parking lot of the baseball field near my house and said he wanted to go down on me, 'You don't have to do anything.'
I laughed, said no.
But the sentence changed it all.

This is why this friendship is hard for me.
Most friendships...
Something nice, followed by that.

When did it start with Alex?
It wasn't always that way?
When I got back from Mexico, 2013 maybe? I was sitting in the very spot I am now, writing a paper for school, wearing little plaid sleep shorts and a tank top. It was sunny, breezy. A spring day. I was grateful some of the shitty windows that could open in my house were open. Alexander stopped over, and we talked about my trip. He said I looked beautiful and tan. After he left, he sent me text messages saying he wanted to eat my pussy. I made a joke back, hoping he wouldn't be like that again.
Eventually, it got to the point I couldn't joke.
Stop or we can't be friends, I told him.
It didn't stop, we stayed friends, but never the same.

I can't share the truth. It will hurt people we love.
And there is no point.
And if I'm totally honest, I get why Alex killed himself. Why I wanted to kill myself.
I cannot write a speech."

∙ ∙ ∙

Sitting in training in Albany, my heart beat fast and irregularly. I was feeling suffocated at the small table I shared with four people I didn't know. I wanted to be silent. Not make small talk. There was no point to that, to the training or what I anticipated was to come the rest of the week: an icebreaker, maybe two truths, one lie again; group activities and exercises, working as a team, writing answers on a flip chart and taking turns reading aloud. The same thoughts raced through my mind: *I don't belong here. I shouldn't be a caseworker. Who am I to try to help? I'm wasting my life, sitting in this room. In pointless trainings. I can't do this. I can't be in this room. I want to quit.*

I felt like I would explode. For a week, I sat like that.

The office wasn't much better. I couldn't be quiet there either. I testified to remove a young boy from his parents then repeatedly in an ongoing case to remove a teenage girl from her mother, winning both. I couldn't see that these things needed to be done, that I was doing a good thing, because my anxiety about speaking and about being alive was so high. It all felt wrong.

In the woods with Broadus, I wished I could just walk forever in silence.

∙ ∙ ∙

Five months after Alexander, I was still drinking too much, exacerbated by summer. On a Wednesday after work, I went with coworkers to Or' for IPAs on the patio, then to meet with Whitney and the rest of the crew after that. Driving home it was dark; the late June sun had already set. Walking into my kitchen, I saw Broadus lying on the dining room floor. Bro was not a floor dog. He had his own chair, the couch, and our bed.

I curled up on the floor, shaping my body to his, hugging him. He felt lethargic, his eyes looked sad, and all I thought about was how much I hated myself for being out and not with him. Again. As he licked my face gently, I whispered in his little gray ear, "I'm sorry, Bro Bro. I love you."

Zak must have prepared the Rav 4, because it wasn't me. The back seats were pushed down in a flat position, Broadus on his blanket. At the vet, I was grateful Zak went inside and spoke for us without asking me if he should. I didn't want to leave Bro for even one second. The vet, Brenda, and a homely technician came out, showing us that Bro's gums were white. They explained he had a seizure, and that blood likely surrounded his brain. They said they could give him medication to make him sleep and pass in the car, comfortably. I didn't think we were coming for this; he had bloodwork done three days prior, it was perfect. He was healthy. I thought they'd fix him.

Broadus shut his eyes and rested. His body slightly and shallowly moved up and down with his breath. I wondered why it was taking so long to work, then wondered what the fuck was wrong with me for thinking that. I didn't want Bro to be gone any faster. I was just so bad at being still.

The technician asked, "Will you take him home or should I arrange for him to be cremated?" It was ninety degrees outside. His dead body would be in the backseat of the hot car. I didn't know where I could dig the hole for him. I wanted him to be somewhere special, by the river or in the park. Not my house. It wasn't special there. What would happen if we moved?

"Cremation," I said and then knew on the way home, without him, that I made the wrong decision. Broadus deserved to be put back into the earth.

Suddenly I was mad at Alexander. If he didn't kill himself, I wouldn't be adding sad on top of sad. I would have been able to make a better selection. Anger felt new to me. But it was gone as quickly as it came. Replaced with sadness, my comfort.

Jamie took the train from Hoboken. I picked her up at the station. Driving up Warren Street she said, "I was thinking about it and maybe Broadus knew you were okay. Maybe it was his time to go help someone else, the way he helped you. Maybe Bro is saving someone else now." A beautiful sentiment. I was not okay though.

Jamie left after the weekend. I tried to go back to normal but hated walking alone in the woods after work. I felt guilty that I missed Bro more than I missed Alexander, but Bro was my constant. He kept me company when I felt alone, traveling from state to state, festivals to dark bars. He protected my soul when Nate and Eddy Vedder destroyed it. I didn't save him from the pound, we saved each other.

. . .

In and out of consciousness at the Half Moon.

I didn't remember going into the bathroom with her. She had small, perfect breasts. I told her that. She said she only wanted to go down on me, for me to do nothing. I let her. She left first.

I didn't remember seeing her or talking to her before the bathroom.

Did she come in behind me? Did we walk in together? How long were we in there? Did Eli or Isaac see me? Zak's other friends too?

I wished Zak had come with us; we begged him to. But I knew it wasn't his fault, it was mine. If I followed my rules, it wouldn't have happened. Plus, this time was different, more than a kiss meant my mistake went further. I had to quit drinking.

The next morning, Zak kissed my forehead. "You okay, love?"

"No. I'm not going to drink anymore."

"Oh. Well, I love you. I'll see you later on my break maybe."

I stayed in bed, my mind wandered, wondering why I hooked up with girls since high school but couldn't imagine dating one. I told myself it didn't matter if I was bisexual anyway, I already married a man. Albeit a man who joked about me being gay, who said he'd be into bringing a woman into our marriage. Into was different than on my own. Without him.

Under my covers, the room lit only from the light of the iPhone screen, I searched sites reading bios of women nearby who were looking for a couple to join. What would we do before? Small talk? And then after? Would we walk her to the door? Stay in the bedroom as she walked out alone? That seemed rude. We'd have to go into another room and hang out with her before saying goodbye. She is a person too. It all sounded terrible. I stopped looking, and again wrote girls off to another thing that only happened when I was drunk. Fix the drinking, fix myself.

. . .

Without alcohol, I drew, exercised, wrote, and walked in the woods alone, but eventually I needed people again.

Whitney's house felt safe.

Barefoot with a backpack full of drinks, I rode my bike there. We played basketball in the driveway, and again inside where a hoop hung on the wall that divided the dining room from the living room. We were careful not to hit her hanging plants; I loved how many she had. I also loved how clean her house always was. Not long ago, before Whitney and Heather broke up, I loved the cupboard full of animal crackers and granola bars too. Helping myself to them felt like home. The snacks left with Heather and her three kids, who I loved too. Replacing them was Whitney's brother-in-law, Jordan.

Jordan was there because Whitney's sister recently left him for their friend and CrossFit coach. The three of us hung out at the house habitually, pretending we were okay, or just trying to be, the best way we all knew how—by standing in the kitchen, drinking while Jordan cooked meat and vegetables for Whitney and me. He ate peanut butter and potato bread sandwiches while we laughed and asked, "Why don't you ever eat what you cook?"

When the weather cooled, I wore new white pants to Whitney's house, drinking too much, I woke up without them in Jordan's bed. Blaming alcohol couldn't touch this wound. I truly hated myself. Hated my lack of self-control. Hated my confusion. Hated that it crossed my mind that Jordan wanted to buy a lake house and that sounded nice. Driving up north with him, spending weekends away, making mini adventures. Having a person.

・・・

Battling telling Zak, I ended up on the side of not.
    I wanted to protect him from pain by keeping the truth to myself. I'd fix it.
    I'd make myself better and never let it happen again.
    It seemed the kindest and only option.

・・・

At work, I looked through pictures, reading self-written excerpts on the *Psychology Today* website, searching for someone who accepted my insurance. I feared the men might not understand me and focused on the women, but no one was jumping out to me as a good fit, or I was overwhelmed by the choices, something that happened whenever I tried online shopping. Eventually, I chose a girl based on proximity to my house. She seemed around my age. Appeared plain. Her name was common, her features softer than mine.

    "Hello, can we schedule a consultation/first appointment? I prefer to be contacted by email, if that's okay," I said. Still not able to speak out loud.

    "Hi Amy, thank you for contacting me. Currently I can offer one appointment every other week at 7:30 PM. Briefly, what areas of concern do you have or what would you like treatment for?"

I responded, "Area of concern... Hm. I guess potential alcohol abuse, marital problems, my friend committed suicide in February. I struggled with depression and being suicidal for about 10 years and never had therapy. I do not feel suicidal now, nor have I in a few years but I continue to make terrible life choices."

"Please ring the bell and wait for me on the porch. The house is blue with white trim."

Waiting there as instructed, I hoped my breath didn't smell like alcohol. If the appointment hadn't been so late at night, I wouldn't have had a few beers at Whitney's.

She opened the door, inviting me to follow her up the three flights of stairs. It was cozy, the ceiling low, the space narrow and long, once a family's attic. She wore a pale sweater with Easter egg colors, confirming my suspicion she might be too nice. My back was sweaty underneath my shirt, pressed against the small loveseat.

"Tell me a little bit about yourself," she said.

"I just have to fix my drinking. Every mistake I make happens when I'm drunk. Then I'll be okay. I mean, I am okay. I don't want to kill myself. So I'm okay," I said and explained a little more.

"Did you experience childhood trauma or trauma at all?"

"I don't think so," I answered, truthfully.

TWO WEEKS LATER she started our second session with a questionnaire, pages of inquiries related to drinking. I knew I failed. Or passed. Depending on how you looked at it. I sent her a text message the day of our third appointment, "I had an emergency and can't come tonight."

"You will still be responsible for payment because it is less than a 24-hour notice," she said.

I didn't pay. Or go back.

In Hoboken, Jamie packed her suitcase while giving me directions to Urgent Care.
"The wait will be a few hours," a young receptionist told me.
"Oh, okay. I can't wait that long but thanks," I said before leaving.

IN LAS VEGAS, Jamie dug through her suitcase that sat open on her bed. I lay in my matching bed next to her searching for my symptoms on the internet.
"I think I found what I have!"
"What?" Jamie asked.
"Shingles."
"You don't have shingles! You're not ninety," Jamie laughed.
"I do! I have all the symptoms, it looks the same, see," I said, showing her my phone.
"Oh my god, you really do have shingles!"
"I know! What do we do?"
Jamie got us a Lyft, which dropped us at the closest Urgent Care. They didn't accept my insurance so we agreed we'd try again at the next stop, then retired to an early dinner at an empty restaurant before seeing *The Beatles LOVE*. We didn't go to bars or casinos like we did last time we visited, for my twenty-first birthday, when Jamie got punched in the face by a man we didn't know and I lost my fiancé, Sam, for days. Then forever.
In the morning, we ate yogurt and granola and joked about how lame we were for having the same thing we did the day before, at the same place. We said we were like little old ladies in our eating routines, going to bed early, and not dressing up like most people did when they visited Vegas.
The last day, we watched Snoop Dog perform in the grassy outdoor arena, passing joints into the audience, a celebration of the legalization of weed, of life. The screen showed a cute

blonde in her early twenties hitting it and I joked to Jamie that she wasn't going to make the Rock and Roll Marathon. But then she was gone, and so too was Jamie.

The strip was cool at night, music played loudly from giant speakers for the racers of the Rock and Roll Marathon. The energy of people on their way to complete a goal almost brought me to tears; I felt it in my throat. As did the heaviness of what I did, who I was. Unable to escape myself, I walked alone through the crowd of people thinking, "I need change. I need a different life."

• • •

The next Urgent Care on our stop closed hours before we arrived, so we headed to the lodge. Opening the door, a man stood near a tall microphone softly playing an acoustic guitar. He was surrounded by mismatched comfy armchairs, people scattered in them, wearing tall wool socks and Patagonia pullovers, red wine in hand. We found where we fit in.

We woke up early, with no alarm.

"Let's go see the sunrise!" Jamie said before we snuck out a side door, close to our room.

Outside, literally steps away, was the Grand Canyon. In all its awe. It had been so dark when we arrived, we didn't see it, had no idea just how close we were. "Wow," I said. "Good thing we didn't stumble out here drunk, we could have fallen right off the cliff!" While we hiked, the straps to my backpack rubbed on the painful rash on my upper right side; Jamie had a cold, tissues in her hand, her nose a little red, raw. We didn't complain. But still my thoughts didn't leave me, how terrible I was.

• • •

We left the Grand Canyon for the Verde Valley to visit Maynard Keenan's winery. At the tip top of the cliff I saw what looked like a castle. "Look at that! Is that where we're staying?" I asked Jamie, who arranged the entire trip.

"It is!" she answered.

The old hospital lived up to its new name, the Jerome Grand Hotel. Grand indeed.

When we arrived in the lobby, which was once an emergency room, we were told about the old spirits rumored to still live there. Little girls and cats that didn't exist who roamed the hallways. A man whose murder was never solved. On our way out of town, back at the base of the cliff, a girl took our order and told us that the town burned to the ground three times. There was hard work and heart in its rebuilding. Her boyfriend, the owner of the café, cooked our eggs in the open kitchen. I admired all of it. The décor was simple, pots and pans hung from hooks in the ceiling, like in an old farmhouse. The counter space took up the majority of the place, leaving room for only a couple tables, making it small enough that the two of them could easily run it, together.

I wanted that.

To live in a cool mountain town.

To own a little café that Zak and I could run ourselves.

Just us.

Serving healthy food that we grew from our own garden in an environment full of positive energy.

Maybe we could still have that, I thought.

· · ·

Jamie made a killer desert playlist and acted as DJ while I drove our rented red Mustang over 100 miles per hour to Sedona. Urgent Care didn't accept my insurance there either. "Can someone just look at my side and tell me if it's shingles? I just want to know what it is."

The receptionist kindly agreed to ask a nurse, who sweetly said, "Follow me to the back."

"Yup, it's shingles," she said, knowing immediately. Adding, "People your age usually get it from stress."

My body could not ignore what my brain shoved deep down.

・・・

The last leg of our tour, I pulled into the parking lot of Jamie's friend's apartment complex. We joked how uncomfortable we felt going in; we shared the same types of anxieties and worried we'd feel weird with them. We contemplated not doing it, "Maybe we should just get a hotel!" Then we reminded ourselves that we always do this, and we are always fine once we get somewhere.

Inside, Jamie's friend told us his wife wasn't feeling well; she had a stomachache and didn't want to be around food. It was just us for dinner.

First, he took us to a rooftop bar, we drank by firelight, looking out at downtown Scottsdale. He took us to a few more of his favorite spots for flights of wine and margaritas.

I came out of my blackout in the middle of doing lines with people. Recollections of doing ecstasy filtered into my mind too. People were coming in and out, buying drugs from the guy. Jamie was sleeping in an oversized chair on a balcony. When she woke up she said, "We have to leave."

I could tell she didn't know what happened either.

"I can't leave yet," I said, infuriating her, rightfully. "I can't go back to the house like this, I can't go to sleep."

But Jamie didn't do drugs, so she didn't understand what I meant and screamed at me, "You're disgusting."

She was crying.

She yelled it a few more times.

She was right, I knew that.

WHEN THE SUN came up, our driver arrived and brought us back. When we walked into the apartment, they were sitting on their couch, watching TV and eating breakfast. I thought, *Really dude, you got us drunk then left us at your drug dealer's house. Fucking nice.*

None of us acknowledged it.

Plus, I knew my actions were my own fault.

Upstairs in their guest room, my heart raced as I tried to force myself to sleep. I felt dirty. Disgusting.

I wanted to die so bad.

· · ·

The next day, our last day, we were scheduled for dinner at the home of Jamie's former boss. She was eccentric and sweet, as was her husband. They taught me that the arm of a cactus can take 100 years to grow. They offered me a glass of wine several times. "Oh, I'm not drinking anymore," I finally answered when they said, "Are you sure?" I left out that it started right then. That my plan to never drink again was my punishment and maybe my savior too.

When our plane arrived back home, I went with Zak to Thanksgiving dinner. His family was shocked I wasn't drinking. I pretended it was to be nice. "It's finally my turn to drive us home!" After seven years of it being Zak's turn, I guess they thought it made sense.

· · ·

Finding it hard to alter myself while my surroundings stayed the same, I slowly returned to my patterns.

I couldn't stop drinking.

Otherwise, I'd be doing everything completely alone.

Broken Gut

While bartending, Zak met a man who called himself "The Count." The Count claimed to be a famous director and found great interest in Zak, who had quit cooking in pursuit of acting. The Count came into Zak's bar a few times before eventually persuading Zak to meet him at a French restaurant.

By the time I was called and made my way across the river to pick Zak up, they had been drinking all day, without food. Zak sent me a text message, warning me that The Count was being crazy but made promises of filming and fame, so we were going to stick around a little bit longer.

The Count made it clear I was not to be a part of their conversation, so I chatted with the bartender instead.

"So, do you like being a caseworker?"

"It doesn't feel like I help as much as I'd like. A lot of the time it feels pointless."

"Why do you stay then?"

"Um. I don't know. I might leave soon. Even though everyone says I'd be crazy to."

"Why crazy?"

"Mostly because of how good the retirement and stuff is. But when I think of staying there for twenty-five more years it makes me want to kill myself! I can't live and work just for that, I could die before retirement anyway. I'm just weird and everything feels pointless," I laughed.

He laughed too, understanding what I meant, and asked,

"Ever read *The Myth of Sisyphus*?"

"Nope!"

"You should! I think you'd like it. It's about meaninglessness and suicide."

"Sounds great," I laughed before being rushed out by Zak when The Count tried to kiss him. Our cue for what he was after.

On the drive home, I told Zak part of the reason it was hard for me to not drink was because of evenings like that, where my love for talking to strangers in bars was reinforced because it provided the connection and conversation I needed.

• • •

The next day, the sun was shining bright as I drove Zak back over the bridge to get his car. "Let's move to L.A.!"

"You'll hate it there," Zak said.

"I won't hate it if we live where I can walk or ride my bike to work!"

"You'll hate the people," Zak said.

"I'd try it! It could be fun. If we hate it, we move back."

"It's not that simple, Amy."

"It is, and then you'll at least know you really tried to be an actor," I replied, imagining him pursuing his art by day and us working in restaurants together at night. Finding our people that way, the way I learned to do in every other city where I knew no one. I pictured us too, on our days off, eating from food trucks, strolling the sunny city with a dog we rescued from the pound.

Having a life.

Together.

• • •

Zak didn't want to move to L.A. or to any of the other places I suggested either. He didn't know how desperately I needed it. That I was trying to run away from myself, an old habit that was hard to break.

• • •

Brushing my teeth before work, I listened to podcasts of people who quit everything to go for their dream. During the day I'd see articles in places like *Thought Catalog* full of the top ten ways to take the leap, "Quit your 9–5." Walking in the woods after work, I'd think how wonderful that must be, to know what you want. To have your gut scream, DO THIS THING. To lack bravery seemed easier than my challenge, not knowing or trusting my gut. It was quiet at best, but mostly it seemed broken.

What would make me feel more alive? I wondered. *Do that,* I thought.

The only thing I both feared and loved was the ocean, so I started there by taking scuba lessons in the pool of a high school gym an hour away. My diving certification was complete when I dove in Lake George on a cold, rainy day. Afterwards, I found information online about becoming an underwater welder. I requested, then received, a packet from a school in Florida. My dad told me of a guy he knew that did search and rescue, usually retrieving dead bodies from the Hudson River. Lou, the owner of the brewery, brought me to his shop for a day, where he welded beer taps.

The shop didn't feel right, so I went for another hike, hoping for answers. In the woods my sight became set on the beauty and craftsmanship of the old stone walls that were abundant in the Northeast, remnants of farmlands from the past. *Leave DSS and learn a trade, that might make me happy,* I thought. Being quiet and building something where I could revel in a finished product in solitude sounded amazing, so I started to ask around.

"You're a stone mason, right? Do you like it? Do you want an apprentice?"

"You don't want to do it. Trust me, it's bad on the body and you have a bad back already," a guy I knew from the brewery told me.

I mentioned it to my dad, who said, "You're a Houghtaling, you can do anything."

His motto.

Within the week he called me back to tell me, "Uncle Louie sends his guys to a masonry school in Maryland."

"Really?" I asked, excited.

"Yup, every February," my dad said.

Nine months away.

I couldn't wait that long for change but had no way to explain that to my dad.

Conversations flowing over a fire at Kaia's house, I continued to talk to whoever would listen about wanting to learn a trade. Finally, a friend said, "Come work for me," and I put my two weeks' notice in, swapping casework for carpentry.

• • •

When I woke up anxious, I quickly got out of bed and put paint-stained pants on. I was relieved to dress like myself. Happy to go to work because work was outside. No matter the weather, that was where I felt better.

Arriving at the property before the other two guys, I sat on stone steps that overlooked the sea of green trees, writing my morning pages: inked hopes of cultivating a new craft, dreams of building a deck at my own house, and fashioning doll houses built from scratch.

Soon after, I learned that the only carpentry I'd experience was cutting wood for floors, which only lasted one afternoon. Mostly, I painted barn doors. Texting Jamie, I told her, "I'm soooo bored. I ate my lunch already, again," because with nothing else to do, it was easy to empty the small cooler packed with a cucumber and hummus sandwich and an apple by 11 a.m.

When the painting was finished, I spent hours watching the other guys sit around smoking cigarettes, looking at their phones. They barely spoke to me and seemed annoyed when I'd try to ask them what else I could do. I hated not knowing the work enough to just pick something up and do it on my own. I tried to stay grateful for my friend who gave me an out and a little bit of hope. But the feeling gnawed at me again, *I'm wasting time. Life is too short for this.*

I MET WITH a friend of a friend at Back Bar. He had black-rimmed glasses and was quirky and super nice. We were meeting to see if I'd be a good fit for the Hawthorne Valley Farm Store. I explained my back was bad from years of dog grooming and more recently from building a stone pathway. Also, I told him I wasn't a baker. Not only for the commercial-size scale like they were, but in general. I didn't grow up baking with my mother. I never asked for or received an Easy-Bake Oven when I was little; I only made spaghetti with Play-Doh. As an adult, I had baked a handful of birthday cakes, cookies, and once cupcakes, for family and friends. That was it.

"Do a trial, see if it works," he said.

"Creating something with organic ingredients from the farm does sound cool!"

The first day, my shift was supposed to end at noon. It was closer to 2 p.m. when I got in my car and drove home, crying a little.

It didn't feel right either.

I felt stupid.

Why did I think I could be a baker?

When I got home, I scoured the internet, learning about yeasts. *I'm a Houghtaling, I can do anything.*

Day two, I made sesame, poppyseed, and everything bagels. Baguettes and loaves of bread. I made square or oblong pizzas, never round, as requested. Day three my back burned from pain, especially when I leaned into the deep sink, cleaning up for the end of the day.

After day three, Whitney and I met for drinks and I explained I sort of wanted to quit already.

"Leaving my house at 3:30 in the morning isn't going to work forever. It's too hard to go to bed that early! And it feels repetitive already. I don't think I can come in and make the same things every day."

"Just say thank you for the opportunity. I can't come in anymore!"

I sent a more professional version of that concept because it was true, and possibly so Whitney and I could continue to drink.

• • •

Scrolling through Indeed felt hopeless. I didn't want a regular job. I wanted more. Or maybe less. I wanted to live fully, but minimally, maybe in the sunshine, near the sea. I went back to looking at jobs where I could camp with at-risk kids. I brought the idea back up of moving to Hawaii and then decided, for the first time since I was sixteen, to take one month off. No job. Enjoy August. Have a minute to breathe.

Most days I rode my bike to Sean's house. I swam, but mostly relished in the freedom of not being a slave to time. Going to bed and waking up when I wanted was refreshing. Working out and walking in the woods felt calmer, less rushed. I slowed down for the first time in as long as I could remember.

• • •

September arrived and I started a job at a nonprofit as a Home Finder. There, I was responsible for recruiting and training people to become foster parents and placing children in homes that were a good fit for them. The hours were a little flexible. There was no time clock. I could work from home some days and make my own schedule. In the winter, they even encouraged me to sneak off for a hike to get daylight hours in. I was hopeful. Excited.

At night, Sean stood in front of me as I sat on the steps near Wunderbar.

"You seem so much happier, Ammers!"

"I am! This job feels right!"

Part of me had always wanted to foster or adopt, and working in that environment was inspiring, regardless of whether or not it would be my forever career.

. . .

Three months later, I laced up my hiking boots and headed into the woods. The snow muted the sound around me as I cried. I cried so hard and wondered what was wrong with me, how I ended up so sad again.

WHEN MY BOOBS were sore, I knew.

I had been there before.

At sixteen, with Sam.

With Nate in Florida.

Those times, back then with them, I assumed it was circumstantial that my depression deepened. I hadn't considered my brain chemistry's capacity to sustain the hormonal change necessary to let me have children. Maybe it couldn't.

Or maybe my mind would adjust and balance out after a trimester or so. Even if it didn't, maybe I'd be saved by the safety that the practicalities were covered—just days away from my thirty-fifth birthday. Married to a man who'd be the best dad.

Health insurance, a three-bedroom house, and suitable jobs. Plus, I always said love was what mattered most to me and loving a child must be the ultimate version of it. A tiny part of me was surprised I hadn't wanted a baby all along.

I imagined the guest room turned into a nursery. I hoped for a little girl. I pictured her wrapped onto me as I climbed through the mountains, showing her the world before tucking her in tightly, reading our favorite bedtime stories.

I kept those thoughts to myself. Both because I was somewhat unsure and because I genuinely wanted to know what Zak felt, without any influence from me. I didn't want to make him have a baby if he wasn't ready.

• • •

My only certainty when I told Zak was, "It's now or never."

"What do you mean?" he asked.

"I'm old! It seems crazy not to do it now when we have no reason not to, then try again in a few years."

"I just need a few days," he said.

LATER IN THE week, I brought it back up. "We kind of have to decide."

"I'm not really ready."

"Okay," was all I said.

PART OF ME was sad and part felt relieved that I could go on operating at the level I had—caring enough to do my part but not vested in the world the way I'd be with a child in it. I understood why my mother told me not to have kids my whole life. "The world is shit," she'd say, and she was right. People were disgusting, concerned more with money than the planet.

It was better this way.
Me, alone.

I CALLED AND scheduled the appointments.
"Should I come with you?" Zak asked.
"You don't have to," I said.
"I could try to get off work or something."
"It's okay," I said.
My primary care doctor, who recently had a baby, glowed as she confirmed I was pregnant. When I said I wasn't keeping it, she tried to hide whatever judgment or disappointment she felt, but it was written on her face. She gave me paperwork, and said I still needed to have an ultrasound. The wait for it was long, even though I was the only person I saw in the lobby. When the lady called me in, she seemed irritated, rude, and as cold as the gel she put on my belly.

The following day at Planned Parenthood, I was told to undress and put the gown on. I did but kept my socks on because I knew I'd need them to protect my feet from the cold metal stirrups.

A light knock on the door, then a small woman came in. Sitting on a swivel stool she looked over my health history as I lay with my head on a flat white pillow.

"Yes, I had two abortions. A long time ago," I confirmed.

"Why aren't you on birth control then?" she said, not super unkindly, but enough for me to feel like a piece of shit.

. . .

Hiking, a thought crept into my head. *What if it isn't my job or where I live that needs to change. What if it is my marriage?* Quickly, I pushed the thought to the place I created inside myself that allowed me to survive—where theories like *you're fat, something's wrong with you, nothing matters, kill yourself* went—and instead said to myself, *Find a new job. A passion. Then I'll be okay. We'll be okay.*

PART TWO

Circa 1983–2004

"Love is the romantic solution to the problem of death."

ROLAND BARTHES

I wondered if I was born sad.

"Mom, was I weird when I was little?"

"No. You were a good baby. You didn't even cry."

A teacher later said, "When a baby doesn't cry, it's not a good sign. It doesn't mean the parents got lucky. It means the baby learned there was no point in crying. The baby gave up."

Misfit Kitten

In kindergarten, I was assigned a seat at the triangle table. Ivy sat next to me. We whispered.
"Fuck."
"Shit."
Giggles.
Instant best friends.

BY THE SECOND grade Ivy and I were sitting in silent solitude, drawing pictures on the thighs of our jeans, while the other children happily sang.
Do your ears hang low?
Do they wobble to and fro?
Can you tie 'em in a knot?
Can you tie 'em in a bow?
Mrs. Knack, glaring at our denim artwork, announced, "If you were my kid and did that, you'd get hit."
"I'd hit you back," I said, my tone calm, dry.
The school principal, out of concern or disturbance, removed Ivy and me from school. We sat in the back seat of his wood-paneled minivan, holding back smiles as he drove us to Bob's diner, a small standalone brick building with an unpaved parking area. From the van I read the sign in the window which advertised "Full Spaghetti and Meatball Dinner, only $5.00." Behind the counter, Ivy's mom served coffee and fried eggs to lonely men sitting on small bar stools. "Bring them back to school, I'm at

fucking work."

A couple miles down the road, we arrived at my dad's shop. The school nurse, sitting in the front passenger seat, apparently there to chaperone two little girls taken out of school by an adult man, said nothing. As the engine idled, Mr. Simpson put one foot on the ground and then quickly pulled it back in when our big black lab came over. "Jack's nice," I told him before they both disappeared between bucket trucks.

The drive back to school was silent and I wondered if my dad was nice too. When it wasn't mentioned at home, I figured Mr. Simpson was told I didn't have to sing. Same as the time he was told I didn't have to wear a jacket if I didn't want to. "If she said she's not cold, she's not cold."

• • •

In the third grade, our class performed in the school play, *The Family Circus*. Because everyone was forced to have some sort of role, Mrs. Knack cast Ivy and me as the characters with the least amount of lines. Before the play began, Ivy dressed in white Fruit of the Loom sweatpants, with a little matching white sweatshirt. I wore the same, but in gray. In the school bathroom Ivy's mother painted little whiskers on our cheeks and colored our noses pink before I scattered off to the auditorium to find my mother.

My mom sat with Nanu and Poppy, my grandparents. Everyone seemed sad, but I didn't know why. When it was our turn, instead of singing, Ivy and I mumbled, "We are the three little kittens who lost our mittens."

• • •

Soon after, my Aunt Karen took me to visit her son, my older cousin Chris, at Berkshire Farm.

Berkshire Farm was a residential treatment program and

school for boys. It had a sprawling campus, with big buildings for school and small cottages for sleeping. The best part was that it was near Queechy Lake. It was here that I found out what happened the day of the Family Circus. To protect Chris my mom told on him for bringing a gun to "the plaza," a colorless collection of concrete buildings: a three-cinema movie theater, Strawberries, Angela's Pizza, Wash Rite, and Hallmark. The local hangout for the cool kids.

I understood why my mom wasn't in the bathroom painting whiskers on my nose, why she seemed sad. It was because my mom loved Chris uniquely and differently than she loved anyone else. Including my sister and me.

"He's my heart," she would say.

This love could have simply stemmed from Chris being the only boy, or the first-born child, to my mother's older sister, Karen.

Maybe, though, it was because my mother had foresight into her sister's unfortunate future.

Quiet

My parents didn't attend church, but my Aunt Karen did. On a handful of Sundays, I went to Faith Christian Academy with her and my cousin Sara. Sara was only four months older than me, but because she'd been to the building so many times, she was the one who led us to the tiny room for bible school, while Aunt Karen went off to be with the adults.

The first few times I was as quiet and unquestioning as I could manage, but by bible class number three, I was told to leave. Instead of going back to my aunt, I went to the playground. Sitting on the swings, I read the lyrics on a brightly colored school bus, "Jesus loves us this I know, for the bible tells me so." Knowing I preferred the monkey bars to the sermons, I thought, *Maybe not me.*

My final straw with Faith Christian came when Chris and Sara, who also attended school there, came home with richly painted portraits of ducks by ponds and streams amongst forests. What was going on over there? How were they producing such similar, beautiful paintings? I never saw them draw or paint at home. Skeptical and envious, wishing I painted them, I made up my mind: I didn't like church.

I did agree to go back once more though, for a Halloween party. Jamie was dressed as Punky Brewster and stood on the auditorium stage collecting a prize. In my purple and black flannel, I watched from below through black plastic-rimmed glasses, bushy eyebrows and a plastic nose attached. I was a bum who got nothing.

∙ ∙ ∙

Sara switched from Faith Christian Academy to Greenport Elementary School in fourth grade, creating a new relationship between us. Prior to that, Sara wasn't allowed to hang out with us much, mostly because Chris said so. Chris had the normal my-sister-is-annoying attitude. But also, Sara always told on us.

The summer between fourth and fifth grade, Sara and I walked from my house, past Faith Christian Academy to West Atlantic Avenue, to meet our boyfriends. The four of us drifted down Rod and Gun Club Road, picking peaches along the way. We settled near a small, secret pond in the woods. With my head resting on my boyfriend's lap, I held my hand above my face, admiring the gold ring with a cursive "A" on it he had given me. We passed a cigarette around, listening to the sounds of the late August afternoon drag on. Sara's boyfriend said, "I heard my parents talking, they say your mom has AIDS."

"No she doesn't," Sara said.

I backed her up, "No. She. Doesn't."

On our way back to my house we didn't talk about it, but I did wonder if that was why Sara always lost the argument with her mom to shave her legs. We both had begged for her to do so, pleading the case by saying Sara was picked on for how hairy she was. We were only repeatedly told to never touch her razor. That was it.

∙ ∙ ∙

The next school year Sara and I spent most afternoons at her house, in the Hudson Terrace Apartments. We ate boxed Kraft macaroni and cheese, played *Donkey Kong* on Super Nintendo, and hung out at Promenade Hill, a tiny park in between the subsidized housing units.

Aunt Karen had a soft, light, milky complexion which

contrasted with her short dark hair; in my mind she was always pale. Even when she took us to Virginia Beach. For as long as I could remember, she seemed as lovely as she did sad. Thin was her baseline, but gradually or quickly she became slightly hollower in both appearance and mood, sometimes.

Other times, she still joked.

"Sara! Amy!" she called from the couch.

Running down, Sara and I yelled back, "What!"

"If you blow in this tube I'll probably fart!"

We laughed, not understanding what the bag attached to her stomach was.

Things felt fine. No one said otherwise.

. . .

Aunt Karen moved into my grandparents' trailer and hospice came to help. Soon after, I was told to go over and say goodbye to her. I walked in the front entryway, which was just a small square of linoleum tile among the brown living room carpet. Aunt Karen was wrapped in blankets, sheets covered the velvet couch. A woman I didn't know left the room. Sitting on a chair near her, I held her hand. It felt like bones, but colder. She couldn't speak, so I didn't either. Forever after, I wished I had.

Too cold to bury her in February, her casket was later carried down the aisle of Faith Christian Academy. The choir sang. A woman read "The Last Waltz," a poem she'd written about my aunt and her last dance with Jesus.

Back at school, my friends said, "We knew what happened when you and Sara both weren't here."

Two years later, those same friends and I snuck out of my house. Heading toward West Atlantic Avenue to visit boys above a detached garage, I stopped in front of Faith Christian Academy. Looking at the white cross that hung as long as the church stood, I thought of Aunt Karen; how no one in our family spoke about her being sick or said she had AIDS. I thought of the other people who died too and how no one talked about that either. Grandma Annie, Dotty, Helen, Buster, Pepper—dead from age or disease. Pete, who killed himself with vodka. Uncle Butch, who shot himself at Olana. Jack, who shot himself too. Kaia's friend Rev, who I knew the least but thought of often because she was a few years older than me and seemed so cool before she sat in a car in her parents' garage and breathed in the carbon monoxide.

"FUCK YOU, GOD," I declared.

"Don't say that, Amy. You don't mean it," my nicest, most normal friend Kat said.

I did though.

Not because I was high or drunk like they thought, but because if there was a god, I didn't like him.

I hated him.

I also knew not to say it again.

I became quiet too.

Joey
Joseph Stanley Kosnick III
Joseph Stanley Kosnick the Third Turd

I remembered my cousin Joey living with his mother only once. The house was on River Road, nicknamed so because it ran along the Hudson River from Albany to their house in Stuyvesant. My first memory of Joey is there. I wasn't in kindergarten yet and he was four years older than me. We sat in his bedroom tying small ropes from dressers and shelves, building GI Joe forts.

Over the years Joey and I continued to build bigger and better forts. At my house, for what felt like hours, we lay in our puffy snowsuits proudly looking up at the ceiling of the functional igloo we built, keeping us warm and silencing the world outside. In the springtime Joey and I, always with the help of Jamie, Chris, and my best friend Hopper, built things too. There was the time, just beyond the tree fort my father made for us, that we found an abandoned school bus. Inside the bus, a motorcycle sat surrounded by junk, including long rolls of plastic. In pairs, we each held an end of the roll and wrapped the plastic around four perfectly distanced trees, creating a clear house among the forest trees.

In Nanu and Poppy's attic, we held Nintendo Club meetings where I was the only paying member, the fee for being the youngest. In their garage we played "bar" instead of house. A VHS tape showed us declaring, "We are the Michelob Ultra gang!" Tired of bar, Joey and I climbed the only oak tree while someone stood near the tall pines, recording us.

Summers we camped on the river every weekend. Monday too, when it was a holiday. On the 4th of July weekend, we gripped sparklers tight in our tiny hands before my father started the real show. All of us stood where the sand met the water, watching the explosions, yelling, "Ohhhh. Ahhh." My mom hollered, "Ey, ey, ey, eyyy," and for the finale, finished with her famous whistle.

Labor Day weekend signaled the end of summer. No more days filled with swimming till sunset, holding ugly contests, catching snapping turtles, riding quads into small trees, swinging from rope swings, or getting caught at other camps because we didn't pay attention to high tide. Over too were nights of freedom, sitting by a fire outside with a marshmallow on the end of a carefully chosen stick, playing cards in the cabin heated by the wood stove, and telling stories in our bunks about the Mole people who lived in the woods behind us. "If you go back there, they'll get ya," the adults warned us.

. . .

Around middle school, Joey's mother went to jail for selling drugs and Joey bounced between houses. He lived with Aunt Lia, our grandparents, and eventually us. Chris already lived there too, so the only place for Joey to sleep was on the couch.

In the middle of winter, Joey yelled, "MOVE!"

"NO!" I yelled back as he lifted me from the couch, carried me to the back deck, and dropped me in a pile of snow, while I wore only a T-shirt and shorts.

On Christmas, Joey drove my brand-new remote-control truck on that same deck. Then onto the cover of our above-ground pool, which ripped open just enough for my truck to sink in, breaking it. Christmas breakfast my dad stood at the stove and cooked us each three slices of Wonder Bread French toast, served with three or four tiny sausage links. Joey and I sat at the stools at the counter next to him and in the way you'd say Chef Boyardee, Joey called my dad "Chef Bigbelly."

Five months after that, Joey and I wrestled over one of those kitchen counter barstools, it flew out of our hands and dropped onto my mom's foot, breaking it before she left for a wedding.

None of us ever got mad at Joey though, it was impossible. For me because he was more like a brother than a cousin. He was sweet and funny and had a beautiful face. Laughing and big when we were little and sad as we got older.

...

On May 8, 1998, seven months before I turned fifteen and one month before Jamie graduated high school, Joey finished work, stopped to cash his paycheck, then told his mother he was going hunting. The next day, he was reported missing.

The posters that went up had a photograph of him standing in our kitchen with a white Pillsbury Doughboy T-shirt on. It had a red collar with a blue banner across the chest. Designed to look like the branding for Tommy Hilfiger, it read instead *Tummy Poke Finger*.

At night, I ran my usual route, and whenever I passed the rumbles of the torn down mill, I thought, "Something happened here." His presence felt strong.

Rumors floated around. First, people said he was killed by kids we camped near, over drugs. Then I heard he lost his mind candy-flipping, disappearing after ingesting a cocktail of ecstasy and LSD. That made more sense to me based on the last time I saw Joey.

He was sitting at my grandparents' dining room table.

"You okay?" I asked.

"Do you hear that frying?"

"What frying?"

"My brain," he said.

• • •

From the living room my dad yelled, "Ame, phone."
"Hello," I said into the receiver.
"Joey told me to call you. He's okay, he's in Florida."
Dial tone.

THE MORE THE years passed, the more I questioned if that phone call happened or if I just wished it did.

• • •

November 2004, six years after Joey went missing.
I was driving home from Pennsylvania for Thanksgiving and told Jamie, "I had the weirdest dream last night. They found Joey in the woods."
"A hunter found a shotgun in the woods off Route 9. The police found a body," Jamie said.
In February we were told it was Joey.
"Foul play is not suspected," the newspaper read.

GIANT POSTER BOARDS full of pictures of Joey were placed throughout the small room in Bates and Anderson Funeral Home. I don't think there was a coffin, or maybe there was a closed one. Or maybe he was cremated and that was there. When it ended, I drove to Florida. Even though I knew Joey wasn't there.
For years and years after his memorial, I still thought of Joey as missing. Which wasn't hard to do because no one ever talked about him killing himself. It took years for me to admit to myself what really happened.

He sat down alone in the woods. With a shotgun. His body rotted for six years before anyone found him.

THROUGHOUT MY ADULT life I always wondered what Joey would be like. What our relationship would be. Would we have stayed like brother and sister? Would he be my best friend? The only thing I was certain of was that I wished he had waited till I was older so that we could have helped each other live or die.

Pretty

SKATE was written in large white letters on the side of the gray tin warehouse that faced Route 9. My mom dropped me off in the parking lot adjacent to it, where giant matching letters read FACTORY. Laces tied together, my rollerblades hung from my shoulder as I met up with Sara.

Inside, skating in endless circles, time was told by what songs played. The beginning—Snow's "Informer." Later, we jumped every time House of Pain said so during "Jump Around." Halfway through, the stout DJ with a frizzy, auburn afro, sat in his booth and announced, "It's time for races!" Competitions complete, the DJ called, "C'mon, grab your partner, get in two rows, facing each other!" Saying it was dumb, we lined up to do the Chicken Dance anyway, smiling the whole time.

Thirsty and hungry, I, Sara, and our group of boys squished ourselves in a small purple booth, eating Gobstoppers and Nerds. To be funny, we sniffed the blue, pink, and purple powders found in the packets of Fun Dip, foreshadowing all our futures.

The night came to a close with a couples' skate. We held hands in the dark to "Bed of Roses" by Bon Jovi, feeling the magic of first crushes.

Standing in the little entryway, near the plexiglass window where you'd pay to get in, I waited for my ride home. A boy who was tall and thin and too old to be there came out and made small talk and then asked, "How old are you?"

"Thirteen," I lied.

I was eleven.

"You look so much older. I was gonna guess sixteen."

"Really, thanks," I said, playing it as cool as I could.

Before I said much more my back was slammed against the wall and the guy jammed his tongue into my mouth. When I pushed him back, he stumbled a little and corrected his anger with a smirk. "What's wrong with you?" he said.

With him gone, I thought about my first kiss, at five. A neighborhood boy who was double my age leaned in without asking, did it, and then pushed me into my lime-green plastic toy box, onto the blue plastic lid. Before that, I loved that toy box, it reminded me of My Pet Monster. Afterwards, I thought of him.

• • •

My dad and Pete grew up together, Stottville boys.

Stottville is a small town, just 4.2 square miles. Families that lived there tended to stay, knowing each other for generations. We were no different.

My mom and Pete's wife were best friends.

Jamie and Pete's first-born daughter Kaia were too.

Soon after, so were Hopper and I.

Hopper was Pete's second daughter, born on February 3, 1982. Exactly to the day, two years prior to my mother's due date for me. By elementary school Hopper and I were already tiny criminals, stealing money from our mother's purses, planning to walk miles to a yard sale that earlier in the day they declined stopping at.

Soon after, we were on bikes, speeding to get strawberry shortcake ice cream bars. Hopper happily ate hers while we inspected the tiny rocks that swam in the open wound on her knee from falling over the shale steps.

While our dads played chess in my backyard, Hopper and I foraged in the woods out front, climbing up and down the steep cliff, finding skulls we swore were human and rocks we knew were diamonds. "If these diamonds are real, they'll cut right through glass!" said Hopper, who, for fun, read the encyclopedia. When we glided the white rocks across the glass panes of the newly installed door to my house and they only scratched surface deep, we knew we were in trouble.

• • •

Hopper lived in the middle of a triplex, Pete's mother Dotty and Pete's brother on the ends. At Dotty's we turned wooden side tables into troll houses. At her uncle's we hid under the covers, looking at *Playboy* magazines. At Hopper's house we played in the basement, making Barbies have sex with New Kids on the Block dolls. We stayed up for days at a time solely to see how long we could go without sleep. Mornings we cooked pancakes with the wrong ingredients, inedible to us, we gave them to Pete. Pete always ate them, either because he was being nice or because he drank handles of vodka, maybe a combination of both. Tired and delirious, in the afternoons we walked up the hill to the Open Gate for snacks. Mary, the owner of the store, looked 100 years old. She was thin, wiry and wrinkly. She looked frail, but we knew she wasn't. When we walked back to Hopper's we sometimes plotted to steal the rolls of money that stuck out from the little square pocket of Mary's button-up shirt. We were never brave, stupid, or mean enough to do it.

Later, Hopper and I created our aliases after throwing bricks through windows at the old L&B warehouse. "If the police catch us, we're Samantha and Jackie Hummore. We're from Canada," we planned to tell the only cop in Stottville, who grew up with our parents.

• • •

On a calm, quiet, windless day, we walked on top of the thick cement railing of the Stottville bridge. Hopper was steps in front of me, dribbling a basketball. Then she was falling, tumbling into the brush, luckily not into the waterfall. Scaling down the ten-foot drop, I yelled, "Hopper, are you okay!"

"Where's my basketball, is my basketball okay?" Hopper yelled.

With my eyes and body covered in poison ivy, I walked to see Hopper the next day. She didn't have a scratch on her.

For the rest of the warmer months, I made sure to keep an eye on Hopper as we descended past that same thick cement railing, through weeds and woods, toward the water. On giant rocks, Hopper stood safely, skipping small stones while I sometimes climbed on the rafters, softly singing the lyrics to my first favorite song, "Under the Bridge," by the Red Hot Chili Peppers.

Two summers later, Aerosmith's *Get a Grip* came out and Hopper and I hung over the edge of the bridge, belting the chorus to "Livin' on the Edge." Tired of that, we trudged to the northern end of the bridge, where a small dirt road led to a circle of trailers that sat surrounding an abandoned, faded pale-green mansion, built in the 1800s. The mansion was rumored to have tunnels in the basement, running through the Stottville creek as part of the passage for the underground railroad. Hopper and I agreed we would live there when we grew up. Hopper planned to invite the boy she loved to live there too. I never met him, but already I knew everything about him. All his favorite things, plus his shoe and pant size. The only request I made was that the giant greenhouse attached to the back would be my bedroom.

Our dreams were demolished though; the mansion was torn down and Hopper's real house fell further apart too.

By the time Pete went to jail for drinking and driving, his belly was already bloated and swollen enough that we could see bright-blue veins through his opaque skin. With him gone, Hopper's mom moved them out of Stottville, killing the bond created by being able to walk to the bridge or playground every day.

We tried to keep it alive though.

We still slept over on some weekends, but it just couldn't be the same. Not only because of location but because of age; we were no longer little kids. Our wild imaginations and inkling to create and find adventure was naturally decreasing and finally, the last shred of it was torn from us when Pete moved into the High Rise.

Once, Hopper's mom or mine dropped us off in front of the nine-story building. The outside was a dull, dirty beige. Inside, Hopper and I rode in an elevator together that smelled like piss. We walked down hallways that felt like hopelessness. We never went back, and Pete died soon after.

My parents had no conversations about it with me. Our families didn't come together for a service or memorial, there were no shared tears. I don't recall Hopper and me having one conversation about it either. We just pushed on, in different school districts with different friends.

• • •

Still trying to fit, Hopper came with me to a sleepover once; a few times, I went with her. On a day when Hopper's sister was away, Hopper invited me to a small get-together at Kaia's house, near the Stottville VFW. I could finally meet Tommy. Hopper loved Tommy.

When Hopper saw us kiss, I attempted to explain, "I swear I didn't know that was going to happen. I'm sorry. I'm sorry." She didn't yell at me or say anything mean to me but I left right away anyway. Walking home I cried for being so stupid, for not seeing it coming. I cried too because deep down I knew what was lost. Summers, birthdays, life.

It would never be the same with Hopper and me again, I thought.

• • •

Friday night, my thirteenth birthday, as I was still struggling with the concept of NOT talking back, my dad's giant hand hit the side of my face, I fell to the pink square of scrap carpet, meant to protect the real living room carpet from black dog hair.

Jamie, who had outgrown letting me go places with her, pushed the passenger seat forward, allowing me to climb inside her best friend's car. Cemetery Road was dark and winding. My window was cracked, the December air cooled the sting on my face. Sitting in the back, sipping a forty-ounce of OE, my thoughts disappeared into the music. "Champagne Supernova" blared through the speakers, which muted their conversation in the front.

The party was thrown by a guy who already graduated. I was in a sea of people I was too young to know. In the basement I poured beer from the keg into a red plastic cup and sat on an old futon. Engulfed in smoke from blunts and Newports, I fell in love with the feeling of it all.

• • •

Weeknights my mom cooked mashed potatoes with some variation of a canned vegetable: peas, corn, or green beans; and a meat: chicken, meatloaf, Shake 'N Bake pork chops. Wednesdays she made her homemade macaroni and cheese, served with hot dogs on white Wonder Bread. My parents ate their dinner in the living room, watching the 6:00 news. When I came home from practice or games, a plate waited for me in the microwave, the meat always cut up into bite-size pieces by my dad. Without heating it up, I'd sit at the kitchen counter, eating before retreating to my room, where I retrieved a hidden two-liter soda bottle from my closet. Where the lid normally sat, I'd place a small amount of foil, piercing tiny holes in it with an earring shaped like a Scottish dog, a Christmas gift from my dad when I was in the second grade. Cautiously, I broke up the weed, placed it on top, and inhaled and exhaled the smoke into the clothes hanging on the metal bar, hoping the closet would mask the smell. Doing my math homework, I wondered how I ever did it without it. Sketching assignments for Mrs. D's class felt the same.

I felt better.

Until I didn't.

The comedown made me paranoid and afraid to leave my room. When I had to, I'd walk past my dad sitting in his recliner, my mother on the couch, both still watching TV. "I have to go wash my face," I'd oddly announce to no one. On the way back to my room, I'd add, "I got soap in my eyes." Explaining why they were red, again to no one.

. . .

Fiona was the definition of cute, she had young chubby cheeks, dimples, and a giant toothy smile. Fiona carried a water bottle with her at all times, before I ever saw anyone else do that. She hated litter and to mess with her, our friends threw stuff on the ground knowing she'd half seriously yell at them, then pick it up. Her best friend Kat was tall, thin, and motherly, in a super sweet way, not an annoying one. Seventh grade soccer season, I joined them and the three of us became a trio. We went to parties in fields, apple orchards, or houses with no parents. We were always the only ones from our grade there.

Calling my dad to pick me up, I felt uncomfortable sitting so close to him on the bench seat of his Chevy truck. *Am I talking too much? He's going to know*, I thought. Keeping my mouth shut, I worried, *Now I'm being too quiet.*

Sober me thought my dad had to know, but for reasons I couldn't figure out, he never confronted me. On that. Which was both relieving and sad. Sad because it created an awkward avoidance between us. Mornings when he drove me to school, he had once quizzed me with "Who sings this?" Now those quizzes were replaced with silence.

We didn't know how to be around each other.

• • •

At my house, Fiona, Kat, and I drank in the basement bedroom, snuck out at night, and smoked weed in Jamie's room, playing Dr. Mario.

"You guuuuys tryyyy thiiiis!" Kat said, handing us an ear from a chocolate Easter bunny and a jar of peanut butter.

"Nooo," Fiona and I said.

"No eating while high!" became our pact.

Aside from lying under a dining room table eating forbidden handfuls of macaroni and cheese, Fiona and I honored that agreement.

FIONA'S HOUSE WASN'T much different than mine, in the sense that her mom never said anything while we smoked weed on the trampoline, ate full boxes of fruity pebbles, and stayed up late listening to the radio, recording "Not an Addict." Her mom blindly picked us up from anywhere without question, always seeming kind of checked out too.

Kat's house was the most traditional, her parents the strictest. They didn't drink, smoke, or fight, at least not in front of me. The family seemed like they went to church on Sundays, or I imagined they did and then sat around while her mother made pancakes from scratch in their cute little country kitchen decorated with everything apple. Pictures on the walls, magnets on the refrigerator, figurines on shelves, collectables lining the tops of cabinets. Literally everything was apples. Kat's older sister's room had Elvis Presley posters and dolls still in boxes. The pool had a deck, surrounded by a plush green manicured yard. Their fluffy white dog ran around.

Still, they were oblivious that the small playhouse they built for their darling daughters became another place to hold our teenage secrets. Games of truth or dare. Listening to mixtapes made by seniors we shouldn't hang out with. The first hand-job I gave to my boyfriend, Bobby. Maybe the first one he received too, based on his expression and embarrassment once outside the shed. "It's just water on my shirt, guys!"

・・・

Bobby was in the eighth grade, only one grade above us. He had thick black hair, bushy black eyebrows, and long black eyelashes that contrasted against sky-blue eyes. Like me, Bobby was a good athlete. We played wiffle ball and basketball together, we swam in his pool. He made other people laugh but not as hard as he made himself laugh, a distinct loud laugh. He bought me weird gifts. For Christmas, a thin gold watch that a ninety-four-year-old lady might wear. For Valentine's Day, the new DMX CD, which had no special meaning to us. His attempts were sweet, appreciated.

Waking up at his house on Mother's Day, his dad drove me home in his pickup truck, pulled over to a roadside farm stand, and said, "Pick out a plant for your mom." A kind gesture given our parents didn't speak.

On New Year's Eve at Bobby's house, my head spun from mixing too much liquor with weed, my chin smashed into the porcelain toilet, bleeding badly before scarring. On New Year's Day, I woke up in the trailer next door. "You passed out, they got scared and brought you over," Bobby's aunt said.

Saturday night, 1997, when I was fourteen years old, most people I knew were at the Pepsi Arena for the best concert ever: The Firm, Foxy Brown, 112, Mase, and Jay-Z. Unable to pull the money together, I convinced my parents to at least give me a ride to Bobby's, where I'd spend the night.

Bobby had the house to himself. He led me to his room, which was lit only by a black light that hung on the wall. I followed him into his neatly made bed. We fooled around like we always did, then went all the way. Afterwards, lying in bed I thought, "If I went to the concert this wouldn't have happened. Not tonight. Not yet."

Next I wondered, *Why didn't it hurt? Why didn't I bleed? What's wrong with me?*

NOT IMMEDIATELY BUT not slowly, Bobby changed.

After practice, in Whitney's bedroom, through the phone Bobby screamed, "You're a fucking slut."

"I know he's my cousin, but he shouldn't talk to you like that all the time," Whitney said.

Knowing I didn't do anything wrong didn't make the words hurt any less.

As I was being yelled at again by Bobby, for nothing, my mother came into my bedroom, grabbed the phone from my hand, and yelled, "I'm the only person that gets to make her cry."

. . .

On my blue bedroom carpet, I sat, my legs folded into an Indian style position, looking at my reflection in the full-length mirror, trimmed with white plastic. I saw the fingers on my right hand gripping the blade from a carpenter knife, carving small, shallow, vertical slits into my left wrist. I thought, *If people didn't think I was pretty, I would've killed myself already.*

I hated myself for thinking it.

I felt fat and ugly.

I knew none of it mattered.

Nothing mattered.

I knew I wasn't allowed to feel that way too.

I had friends.

I was an athlete.

It wasn't my mom who died. Chris and Sara could be sad, not me.

. . .

I expressed that I wanted to die to one person—my friend Lucy. Lucy and I were in the same grade, but she wasn't allowed to hang out with me outside of school because her mother thought I was a bad influence. Sometimes though, her father brought me home from games. Likely it was kept a secret, probably one of several in her well-known, upper-middle-class family. Full of educators and coaches. Lucy followed in their athleticism too. She was the star of every sport we played together: soccer, softball, and basketball. Lucy jokingly said I was like "Go Ask Amy," a play on the title of a book we loved, *Go Ask Alice*.

Alice died in the end.

• • •

Like Alice, I kept a diary. In addition to thoughts though, mine included secret codes that kept track of the days I:

Drank *(D)*,
Smoked weed *(S)*,
Drank and Smoked *(D/S)*
Wanted to kill myself *(K)*.

At the end of the month, I tallied the totals, searching for a correlation between using and being sad, searching for an answer to *What is wrong with me?* The journal also listed what exercises I did in detail, often running in the dark after practice, then doing sit-ups in my room. Motion diminished the depression for a moment. Not enough to control myself though.

When I broke a girl's nose in the locker room at an away basketball game, my coach sent me flowers with a tiny square card attached that said she was upset I couldn't play anymore—I had potential, as a player and a person. I was grateful for her compassion and remorseful about letting her down. Later she told me she didn't think I was bad, just impulsive. My soccer coach said I was "the toughest player he coached."

I didn't feel those things. I cut class out of necessity and cried in the girl's locker room. I was caught passing a bowl back and forth in the school bathroom with Sara because I was living in my head and smoking made it better, for a moment. A risk I was willing to take. Even after that, when the school ordered me to see a drug abuse counselor, I wasn't quiet with the counselor to be rebellious. I wanted to tell her everything. I just didn't know how, so I said nothing. Alone in my bedroom though, I looked at my journal and thought, *Just bring it...tell her to read it.*

I went to the second session empty handed and after it ended, in my mom's SUV in the parking lot, I could tell from the redness and puffiness of her eyes that she'd been crying. *She's mad at me. Embarrassed,* I thought.

"I'm not going back. It's stupid," I told her.

YEARS LATER, WHILE my mom stirred something on the stove, she said, "I never said anything back then because I thought it was my fault something was wrong with you."

It made me sad she thought it was her, when I knew so strongly, it was me.

Saved by Sam

Bobby's older brother was friends with Sam; suddenly Sam was sleeping at their house too. Drinking at the gravel pit across the street, the guys mockingly called Sam's girlfriend "Saratoga." Maybe because she was from there, but I didn't think so.

Sam's dirty-blonde hair was covered with a blue baseball hat that matched the hue of his eyes; a barbell-shaped earring pierced through his brow; rings were in his ears. He always layered his shirts. When it was warm, he still wore two. Slivers of white fabric peeked out under his gray T-shirt sleeves, and near his collar too. His pants were baggy, but not too much. The black laces to his wide DC skateboarding sneakers were loose, never needing to be tightened because Sam never walked in a hurry. Sam was funny, but not the typical Hudson humor—his jokes weren't at the expense of others. He was kinder and smarter than that, or Sam simply had the good fortune of not growing up in the small towns that surrounded me.

Right outside of Hudson, in the woods of Claverack, Sam, Fiona, and I left the warmth of a fire. The light faded and then finally far enough away, the voices of our friends disappeared too. Arms entwined, the three of us stumbled onto the dark paved road. We walked to the corner of Old Lane, where a large white farmhouse stood, slightly out of place amid regular raised ranches, but welcoming. "I'm just staying here till graduation," Sam said, opening the front door to his aunt and uncle's.

"Where's your parents?" I asked.

"Illinois."

"Oh, is that where you're from? Before Hudson?" Fiona asked.

"Cherry Hill. New Jersey," he responded, without offering up any more information.

Fiona filled the air with chatter, but I didn't hear what she said. My attention already shifted toward my right hand that slowly glided up the thick wooden rail of the staircase. Decelerating time. Steps felt endless upon our arrival to the second level, where small bedrooms, reserved for Sam's four cousins, connected to a family room. Sam set us up there, turning on a tiny television, placing blankets on the couch where Fiona fell asleep fast, leaving no room for us to sit. Coercing us to curl up with quilts on the floor.

Sobered up enough, I knew we had to be quiet.

Never did I say, "Stop."

During sex, I didn't say, "I don't want to do this anymore."

Although I thought it the entire time.

When he was done, I wasn't mad at him.

He didn't do anything wrong.

He was nice. Nicer than Bobby.

I liked Sam.

But now I knew Bobby's intuition was right.

I was a slut.

· · ·

I sat on a closed toilet seat, eating the pills from a fat, full bottle of Advil, trying to untangle what happened. A silent rage of confusion swirled inside of me. *Why didn't I leave Bobby before Sam?*

His words were poisonous, painful.

Not always though.

I loved him, that's why I stayed.

Bobby doesn't deserve this. Do I tell? How? What about Sam? That wouldn't have happened if I wasn't drinking. Do I need to stop drinking? I can't do that. That's already who I am, I thought.

At least one piece of the puzzling question, *what is wrong with me,* was answered.

I was a cheater.

The type of person everyone hated.

Unforgivable.

A tangible reason for wanting to die.

. . .

Sam seemed happy about what happened, about us.

He came to my softball games. I hit multiple home runs. I seemed happy too. Walking with me to the locker room Sam said, "I played baseball when I was little."

"Why'd you stop?" I asked.

"My dad was a dick."

His father, a former football star, left little Sam all alone on the field, dirt flying up as his tires spun fast. Mad at nothing important. Sam didn't play sports after that. Instead, he drew. He showed me soulful eyes he penciled on paper, his portraits of people were beautiful and somehow sad, like him. Sam tried to deflect it by being blasé. He made weird, funny faces in every photograph taken of him, but I saw who Sam was.

Standing amid the school's art, displayed in the open gym, Sam said, "Without knowing, I picked yours as my favorite." My black and white etching of a man sitting slumped over at the foot of the falls, only his canoe beside him. Alone. Sam saw me too.

. . .

Bobby and I had conversations full of anger and tears. Yelling and love. We knew what we were to each other. So many firsts. We also knew what we did to each other. His words, my actions.

In my yearbook he wrote, *"We have been through a lot this year, good and bad. I'm always here if you need me."* Simple, sweet, forgiving. Reminders of why I loved him; why I hoped he was relieved to be going into the eleventh grade single, afforded the opportunity to be with normal, happy girls. Not me.

Sam wrote things in my yearbook too. First, things that made me laugh. Then he ended with, *"I think the world of you, with all of my heart I do, blood through my veins for you, you alone have all of me. I will wait for you, I will wait for no one but you. You know we danced in the risk of each other, would you like to dance around the world with me? That's that Dave shit. I'm so in love and you are the sweetest thing. I look forward to every time I see you. That one night when we were real drunk and had a real good time, that was a beautiful night and I'm glad we shared that. Anything you ever need, I'll give you. I will always be right here. I love you with all my heart and soul."*

A beautiful night we shared.

• • •

Sam invited me to go to work with him. We watched movies in the back of the shack-sized store, located at "the Claverack light," an intersection where 9H and 23 met. Sam only left me to stand behind the counter, taking money from customers in exchange for DVDs rented. On a Sunday Sam had off, we drove forty-five minutes away to the town of Woodstock. Trapped in its time, Grateful Dead Bears and tie-dyed everything splashed shop windows. Inside, the aroma of Nag Champa smoke filled the air as we browsed through old albums and admired handmade stone jewelry. When Sam sat on a swivel stool, I stood browsing sheet art on the walls behind him. A shirtless child with wild, honey-blonde curls ran around us. His head tilted back, laughs coming from his belly as he occasionally called out, "Ma!" to the woman with matching hip-length hair who tattooed the Chinese symbol for "Love" on Sam's forearm.

Monday, the end of my freshman year, I wore a full-length, flowy skirt with a thin-strapped black tank top, revealing the tribal sun between my shoulder blades.

"Woah, you got a tattoo! That's not real!" Kat said.

"Why a sun?" Fiona asked.

"No real reason. I just picked one," I said, knowing nothing lasted or mattered.

Not my body.

Not me.

. . .

Frank was husky, his thin mustache frowning under blue, beady eyes buried behind glasses. The top of his unbuttoned flannel exposed a necklace that sat too tight to his thick neck. I was told Frank was extremely smart, "wasting his IQ," too. I wouldn't know it firsthand though because Frank didn't engage with me in any real way. He wasn't overtly mean, but I could tell he only spoke to me as Sam's best friend. Not because he wanted to.

Frank's girlfriend was a year his senior. She was around five feet tall, her dark dirty-blonde hair half that. Beach-like waves, natural. She was chubby and sweet and never complained as she drove us around, everywhere. Mostly to Frank's house. A brick row house on lower Union Street where beer was the only beverage and black mold lined the bottom of their shower curtain. Not dirty but lived in.

Frank's father was an older man who lit a cigarette before the cigarette in his mouth was fully smoked. He and Frank's mother, Sue, ran their own business. Sue stood on a ladder, wearing overalls with a paint can in her hand and a cigarette in her mouth too, her voice as raspy and worn as she was tall and thin. She drove around in an old pickup truck, their yellow lab riding shotgun, not giving a fuck. Frank's sister, Hattie, followed

Sue's suit in appearance and in nature.

Most nights, Hattie had at least one friend over. They were four years younger than me, but I liked—even preferred—them. Hanging out in Hattie's room one night, high on ecstasy, I playfully hit them with a giant purple and yellow stuffed snake, won from the Columbia County Fair. "SSSS," I said, all of us laughing. Before bed, they made me toast, feeding my drunkenness with the few food options in the house while I secretly grieved for the girlhood they still had, and also for them, because I knew growing up in this town, in this house, it was a short matter of time before it ended for them too.

Outside of Hattie's room, handfuls of kids piled into the kitchen. We played asshole, kings, and bounced quarters off the small table, aiming for the cup in the center. Everyone was connected not only by age but by memories made since grade school. All of them at ease, effortlessly themselves with each other. Besides my relationship with Sam, I was acutely aware I didn't belong there, especially with the girls. I noticed how unanimated I was, how low the volume of my voice was compared to theirs. I wondered if Sam wished I were more like them. Bubbly. I knew I did.

Drugs brought me closer to it, a self I liked better.

Alcohol especially quieted the inner voice allowing me to be funnier, undone.

Morning revealed the truth though. Or what felt like the truth when I was too young to understand what coming down was. Too young to see that my self-perception was altered while substances wore off and my body fought to restore chemical imbalances. To teenage me, my heightened anxiety and depression simply seemed like deserved consequences for blacking out. The not remembering caused shame and self-hate, not the drugs and alcohol.

Remembering created it too.

Being slammed into a brick building in the alleyway between

Frank's house and Allen Street by my friend, I told myself it wasn't a big deal; it was only a forced kiss, luckily nothing more. I tried to forget it too when guys who were supposed to be my friend, Sam's friends, secretly requested, "Give me a real quick blow job." My saying no didn't matter to them, they still called me a slut anyway.

Loving Sam only slightly diminished how much Hudson made me want to die.

. . .

At the Claverack Firehouse, a long, narrow, tan folding table held three labeled baskets. Two of them were overflowing with envelopes, presumably cash-stuffed cards that read "Congratulations! Class of 99!" Sam's basket, the third one, was barely filled. We said nothing about it as he took my hand in his and led me away, keeping me by his side all night. While we watched a girl sing "God of Wine" to a boy who no longer loved her, I wondered if Sam felt safer now too, like I did. Happy to have a person to be muted with.

Later, Sam took me to a girl's house who graduated a few years before him. Near the courthouse, we climbed through her kitchen window onto the fire escape, smoking and drinking the night away. Inside, she fried perogies on the stove before walking toward the bathroom with Frank.

"You don't have to come with us," Sam whispered to me.

"I know," I said.

"You shouldn't."

This was the second time I knew Sam was going to do coke. The first time was at Frank's, when Sam said, from behind an already locked door, "You can't come in."

This time it was up to me.

Without reservation, I followed.

In addition to parties, that summer brought festivals too.

Sam parked his Ford Taurus at the Oswego County Airport. We walked through the lot where people poured acid out of Visine containers and sold nitrous balloons for five dollars. Everyone was free spirited and friendly. It felt contagious and I couldn't help but feel that too.

I ate some sort of pills with Sam and said, unconcerned, "I can't feel my legs!"

"I can't either!" Sam laughed.

"Where's the car?" I asked.

"Let's look for it!"

Time felt infinite as we floated through the lot before Sam finally said, "There it is!"

"What did we need out of it?" I asked.

"Nothing!"

Laughing, Sam placed an orange road cone on the roof.

Finding the stage, we heard Phish play the last few songs of their Sunday set.

The following weekend we drove to Rome, New York for Woodstock 99. I was fifteen.

People seemed okay, but not quite as nice as the last time—sharing less, charging more. Especially the vendors. Food and water were expensive enough that we only bought one meal, which Sam and I planned to split but ended up dumping because it was too hot to eat in the constant 100-degree heat. Minus the misting tents, there was no shade anywhere to be found. Sam and I gave the rest of our money to men for ecstasy, which only worked half the time, and nitrous balloons, which worked every time, but only for a few minutes.

Saturday, two days after arriving at the festival, I was lifted on top of the crowd of people, surfing above men who grabbed at my breasts and tried to slip fingers inside me. Kicking to get down, I couldn't. When I reached the front of the stage, a security guard lifted me over the wall, allowing me to walk back in an area closed off from the crowd. Back with the masses, a man my dad's age asked, "You okay?"

"Yeah, just looking for my friends."

"Come to my RV with me, I'll help you look after," he kept saying before grabbing my arm and pulling me hard, until a young couple intervened and yelled at him to get off of me.

Tired and lost, I sat down on a dusty, dirty curb, defeated. The feeling was diminished when a stranger handed me a bottle of Nestea. "You look like you need this more than me." I did. It tasted better than anything I had ever had before. Unable to savor each sip like I knew I should, I devoured it.

Finally finding our tent, I waited there alone till Sam returned.

"I made a song while you were gone," he told me. Then he sang low and lightly, in a speaking voice, "Where oh where can my Amy be? The crowd surfed her away from me"; cute and clever, crafted from the Pearl Jam song, "Where oh where can my baby be, the lord took her away from me."

We didn't talk about how long I had been lost or what happened while I was gone.

On the last day, frat boy fans became angrier, flipping cars right in front of me. Fires in towers behind. On the drive home, the childish sense I'd had, "I should've been alive in the sixties," was gone, so too was the hope for finding a culture to connect to.

Still in the car and almost home, I said to Sam, "Let's rent a movie." At the video store Sam put two quarters in the machine out front, turned the knob, and handed me the plastic bulb that popped out. Opening it, there was a tiny, blue rubber ninja. "Aww. I love him," I said. "I love you," Sam said before buying me three more. At home, I lined my little ninjas on my dresser, showered, and climbed into the comfort of my bed. Trying to sleep I said to Sam, "I can't without my fan. I need the noise."

"Go get it, it's yours."

In Jamie's room I asked for it back.

"No! You left," she answered.

"I didn't move out. I was just gone for the weekends," I said.

"Too bad."

Knowing she didn't need a fan to sleep, I unplugged it.

Our voices got loud enough that my father cornered me at the end of the hallway, in Jamie's doorway. I tried to explain I was taking my own fan back but, again, it was construed as me talking back. Before I was finished with my side of the story, my dad's giant hand was hitting my face. Pissed off, my mom came too. She grabbed the fan and marched down the hallway. We followed her through the dining room, the kitchen, then outside to the deck. We watched her throw it into the yard, breaking the cage that protected the blade into pieces.

"Sorry," Jamie whispered.

My parents said nothing.

Sam promised, "Two more years till you graduate, then you'll move in with me."

LESS THAN A month later, Sam left for the fall semester at the Chicago Art Institute.

I was alone again.

• • •

Weeks later, on Cemetery Road in a big, bare kitchen that belonged to two older guys and a Saint Bernard, Frank introduced his new college friends to the circle of people standing there. He started with the person closest to him and proceeded in order saying everyone's name, till all were introduced, except me. Only I was skipped over. My name not being mentioned made me more mindful when other people stood directly in front of me, blocking me, speaking over me.

Unable to determine why that was happening, I set out to decipher what was wrong with me in general. In my notebook, I made a correlation between feeling weird and self-conscious to smoking weed. I'd be more conscious; I'd take better notes, I told myself after I went home early from a party in the woods because I got high and thought, *Shorts...I'm too fat to wear shorts. Flip flops. Look at my feet. I'm so ugly. Why am I here? I don't want to be anywhere.*

In the morning, I wrote that I'd smoke less. Or stop.

I wrote too, "I have to stop hanging out with Sam's friends. They are not my friends. I need change."

• • •

Tenth grade, even the good kids my age started drinking and smoking. While I was used to partying mostly with Kat and Fiona, now I had Ivy again too. Ivy and I never stopped being friends since kindergarten, since the triangle table—but I hadn't hung out with her outside of school in years. It felt better to be around her. Around my peers. I understood acutely that I had underestimated the importance of being with people my age. Boys included. They wanted the same thing from me but went about it in a harmless way, never forceful or mean.

This was why I wasn't worried at all when my one girl friend and I went to a house with a handful of boys from my grade. It seemed safer, which is why I was genuinely surprised that I ended up with Braden, my elementary school best friend, in the master bedroom of the house. We shut the wide wooden doors and I could hear the other boys giddy outside, trying to listen, laughing with boozy excitement that one of them was actually going to lose their virginity.

The next day, when Braden asked me to come walk with him, I worried he regretted what had happened the night before. Besides being beautiful, Braden was wholesome and better than me, but too sweet to say or know. Instead of politely throwing me away, he held my hand through his neighborhood. "Remember how obsessed we were with little dog statues in second grade?" I said.

"Yes! Remember when you gave me a tree frog for my birthday! We were so weird," he laughed.

"It was more weird when we used to smell each other's armpits," I said, feeling like maybe things could be okay for me.

Back at school on Monday, Braden's ex-girlfriend Brittany confronted me. "Braden and I should have been each other's firsts. I can't believe you did that." Brittany was beautiful too, her family nice and normal, and I knew she was probably right.

At night, Sam called. "Someone told me they saw you holding hands with Braden Saturday."

"I'm so sorry," was all I could say, truly meaning it and not understanding myself.

How could I love Sam and like Braden too?

"You shouldn't talk to me. Something's wrong with me. Just do what you want at school," I said, not wanting to hurt him or anyone else again.

"I'll buy you a train ticket for winter break, we'll be okay," he said.

• • •

Sitting in the Rensselaer train station, Jamie said, "Mom, did you see the cuts on her wrist? Look."

My eyes met my mother's briefly before we both looked away and I pulled my sleeve further down to protect us both. If any of us spoke again before people began to board the train toward Chicago, it wasn't about anything consequential.

"Bye, love you," I said and she did too.

ON THE TRAIN, my charcoal pencils were splayed out around me.

A man sat in the seat across from me. "Whatcha drawing?"

"Nothing," I said, too embarrassed to share.

"Let me see," he said, gently reaching for my notebook. "These are good!"

"Not really."

"Don't say that. They are."

"It doesn't matter though because I don't know how to draw my own things," I said, showing him torn-out pages of models who posed for advertisements in *Glamour* and *Cosmo*. "See, it's not really mine. I can only draw what I see. It doesn't count."

"I think it counts. Mind if I write a poem in it?" he asked.

I let him leave his beautiful words of desolation and depression on the page before he departed to Buffalo. Shortly after he was replaced with two girls, maybe in their mid-twenties. Based on their behavior and bronzed brown hair, I'd guessed they were sisters or best friends. They seemed fun, I thought, while drinking one of the bottles of Robitussin I brought. Sleeping away any reminder of who I was.

SAM MADE ME feel safe, he guided me through the Chicago streets, holding my hand tight. When the rain started and didn't stop for a day, we stayed in bed listening to albums play. When the sun came out and the wind was strong, Sam brought me to a small, off the beaten path place. We ate cheesesteaks, which he claimed were the best in the city. He was not wrong. At night, we gave money to people who tried to sleep on grates to catch some heat. After we went to the theater to see *Girl, Interrupted*, Sam softly wiped a tear from my cheek as I silently wondered, *Do I have borderline personality disorder? Do I belong somewhere like that?*

Sam brought me to parties. At one of them I said, "Every girl here is so beautiful. So tall. So thin. So interesting."

"They aren't real girls!" Sam said as I was being pulled away.

"Girl, we are bringing you to the Barbie room. You are getting your picture taken," one woman said. With her and her friends, I admired their inclusiveness, originality, and depth. They gave me hope for a world outside of Hudson.

The last few nights, Sam said he had tickets for us. First, a hockey game. At the gas station we chose the largest cups we could find, filling them halfway with ice and fountain Coke, leaving the rest of the room for rum. Arriving at the venue, a man laughed, "Guys, the game is tomorrow!"

Warm from alcohol, and not enough money to take public transportation to the dorm, we walked until we were freezing. Wandering into a hotel for warmth, we took the elevator to the highest floor, which was some sort of ballroom overlooking the city. Sam pressed me against the tall wall made of windows, undressing us both. When the lights turned on, a small group of people stared until one said, "You cannot be doing that in here." As I pulled my clothes on Sam held his pants in front of him, talking for both of us. Apologizing.

At the police station we stupidly offered seats for the Bulls game the next day as the officer said, "Yeah, we're going to need to see ID."

Sam showed them his.

"I'm only fifteen. I don't have one."

"We can have you arrested for statutory rape," they told Sam before calling my mother at 4 a.m. "Hello, ma'am. This is the Chicago Police Department. I'm sorry to call you so early in the morning. Did your daughter run away?"

My mom must have said no, because they let us go.

THE DAY I left, Sam gave me my Valentine's Day gift—a stuffed sheep dog, literally as big as me. At no extra cost, the sheep dog had permission to have the seat next to mine. For the twenty-three-hour ride home, I slept on and off, snuggling my stuffed dog, knowing I couldn't wait two more years to leave Hudson.

I wouldn't make it that long.

∙ ∙ ∙

For the next few months, Sam tried to continue forgiving me for what I had done with Bradey, but the distance between us made it hard for him to trust me.

I didn't blame him.

I didn't trust myself either.

I continued to drink and do drugs and count down the days until tenth grade ended.

Dirk

Dirk had been to my house before, at parties thrown by my cousin Chris on the weekends when my parents slept on their boat. By thirteen, I had already said no to giving Dirk a blow job, but that didn't mean I wasn't attracted to his bad boy persona.

Now, at fifteen, just days after Sam called to say he had to end things between us, I was in Dirk's childhood bedroom.

Our bare bodies were pressed against each other as he pouted his full lips, then smiled, flashing dimples the way he did when he wanted something, "Go get us loosies," he said. Even though he was old enough to buy cigarettes, and I was not. As I slipped clothing on, he leaned over, took quarters and dimes from the night table, and handed them to me.

The walk was quick from his house to State and Third Street, the closest corner store. Returning to his room, I had to pass through the kitchen, where his mother was. She was up, assumingly rested from a normal night of sober sleep, unlike me. Her voice was chipper, and I wasn't ready for any of it.

"Oh! You're a Houghtaling," she said. An undeniable fact.

"Yeah," I said, hoping that looking like my father wouldn't get me caught again.

"Johnny's daughter?"

"Yeah."

"Your aunt, Lia, is one of my best friends! We all partied together!"

"Oh, cool," I said, understanding she wasn't telling on me.

In Dirk's room he pulled me back into bed with him. Wrapping me close he whispered, "Stay."

"I can't, I have finals."

His house sat on a dead-end street where steep cement stairs led from the road to an abandoned little league field. Climbing down, I cut across the overgrown green grass toward the wooded bike path, avoiding human contact, focusing on one thought, *Don't kill yourself. Two more tests, then tenth grade is over. Make it that far.*

Sitting in the small metal chair, coloring in bubbles with a pencil, my left hand glided over my ribs, then past my stomach, which felt gloriously flat and empty without real food for days. My head felt empty too though, I needed sleep.

The blinker beeped, signaling to go left out of the school parking lot as my mom said, "Sam called. He told us what you're doing."

"I'm not doing anything," I said.

"We're not stupid, Amy."

If I hadn't been on a binge, I might have felt relief that my mother and father knew the truth. Or scared. Instead, I felt hollow, so I said nothing more, and neither did my mother. The silence made the seven minutes it took to get home feel eternal.

"What did you tell them?" I asked Sam once I was alone in my bedroom and able to call.

"The truth. You're doing coke. Not going to practice. Fucking up your life."

"Why would you do that?" I asked.

"You know why. Look who you're hanging out with. That's who you want to be like," Sam said.

Again, I didn't have words, so I cried.

Sam said not to. "I didn't tell to hurt you, I told because I still love you."

"I know," I said.

"I don't care that we're broken up, come live at my mom's with me. Get away from Hudson, get better."

Since Sam had already stopped attending the Art Institute, he agreed to pick me up right away. I don't remember saying goodbye to anyone, not friends or family, only that I curled up in the front seat of Sam's car, using my backpack full of clothes and Bunny as my pillow, and slept almost the entire twelve hours it took to get back to Sam's small suburban town, fifty miles outside of Chicago.

Years later, Jamie told me that she called home from Fordham University the week I left. She said she spoke with my mom like normal, about nothing in particular, then asked what I had been up to, where I was.

"What did she say?" I asked.

"That you moved to Illinois!"

"That's it?" I laughed and asked, "What'd you say?"

"I was like, what do you mean she moved? What about school? Why did you let her do that?"

"What did she say?" I laughed again.

"Nothing. You know how they are," Jamie said.

"Oh that's funny," I said, but thought that maybe on some unspoken intuitive level, my parents knew I wouldn't have made it if I stayed in Hudson too.

Seven-Year Stretch

We left Illinois less than a month after arriving, following Sam's sister and long-time boyfriend to a nice but mundane apartment complex on Sauerkraut Lane in a place called Macungie, Pennsylvania. In the stark, white, small second bedroom, Sam and I set up a black futon on a metal frame and unpacked nothing else before driving ninety-six miles away to East Rutherford, New Jersey. It was near Sam's birthday, a hot but breezy July day. Sam wanted to spend it at Giants Stadium, seeing the Dave Matthews Band, his favorite. We arrived mid-afternoon, set up camping chairs near the trunk that held our cooler; Sam assembled a tiny grill and cooked frozen pretzels and hot dogs for dinner. Buzzed enough, Sam took the two tickets from the glove box, stuffed them in his shirt, and extra beers in the cargo pockets of his shorts so that we could wander the lot, buying as many balloons as we could. With the last cash we had, we half seriously argued over who would have the final one first.

Sam inhaled the clear nitrous oxide into his body. On the exhale he slumped slightly over, forehead and chest parallel to the pavement, his feet staggered three slight steps before his head slammed into the hitch of a truck. The balloon released from his hand, before I had my turn.

Kneeling next to him I placed my hand on his chest, saying his name over and over while a crowd of people stood around us, some laughing. A handsome bearded man knelt to our level. "It'll be okay," he told me.

Sam opened his eyes, sat up fast, and said, "What the fuck," pushing the bearded man away from him.

"He was just trying to help," I said as the man walked away, understanding Sam's pride was what was wounded.

Sam disappeared quicker than I could keep up and I found my way back to the car. With no keys to get in, I sat on the hood because after Woodstock, one of my biggest fears was to be lost. After what felt like hours, I accepted Sam wasn't coming back to be with me. He was inside. With both tickets. Bored, it seemed safe enough to roam around the lot as long as I kept my eyes on where we were parked.

When I found a group of kids with no tickets like me, I told them what happened with Sam.

"Fuck that guy, you need this," a girl said and handed me a bottle of tequila that I drank straight from the bottle.

When the bottle was gone, they shared beers with me. As I stood on a giant blue plastic cooler drinking one, an officer came over and said, "Get down from there. We need to see ID."

People produced them.

Except me.

"Where did you get this," one of the two officers demanded, taking the can of beer from me.

"I brought it," I lied, not wanting to get my new friends in trouble for serving someone so young.

On the stadium property, I was brought to a makeshift medical tent. Cots covered in cream-colored sheets were lined in long rows. A lady guided me toward the end of the cloth wall. "Lay down here," she said, kindly.

I sat instead and stared at the people around me who appeared comatose.

"How much have you had to drink? Did you take anything else?" the lady asked.

"Only a couple of beers," I said.

She took my temperature, then checked my heart rate and

said, "We're going to help you. It's okay, honey. I'll be right back, it's okay."

I don't recall getting up or pushing the tent wall open enough to get out, just the vision of running, looking back briefly, the white, bright tent contrasted against the night sky behind me. There was no relief from being away because I quickly understood I had been taken too far from the car.

I was lost.

Nothing looked familiar and everything looked the same.

Eventually, long lines of cars began to form, waiting their turn to go home. People offered to help me, until there was almost no one left.

"We'll get you back to Pennsylvania in the morning," a nice girl told me.

She sat in the front with her boyfriend. I was squished in the back with three other guys. We drove until we arrived at a house, very close by. They pushed the coffee table against the couch, making room for me to lie on the living room floor. Blankets and pillows were given to me. Drifting to sleep with my sneakers still on, I could hear them laughing in the kitchen.

My eyes opened to a man unbuckling my pants, "I have my period," I said, quickly. Because it was true and because I was too naïve to understand it wouldn't make a man necessarily stop.

"I don't care," he said.

Pushing him off, I left in the dark.

In a McDonald's parking lot, I stood in a booth that held a payphone and cried for what felt like forever, until a woman with wrinkles and a silver bun consoled me. "I'll bring you home," she said, again and again.

"I don't even know how to get there," I cried more.

"What do you live by, dear?" she asked.

"Lehigh Community College," I answered.

I saw Sam's sister as soon as I walked in. She immediately said, "When I saw Sam sleeping alone, I tried to get him up. I shook him, saying, 'WHERE'S AMY?'"

He was too out of it to answer her in the middle of the night, or maybe even early morning. When I went in, he was still asleep. Shaking him awake, I said, "You left me in another state and went to sleep."

The next show Sam left me at, I sat on the hood of the car again. My back pressed against the windshield, looking up at the sky, I knew not to leave.

• • •

Sam's sister yelled at him from the bathroom, "You can't just stop taking these, it's dangerous. The doctor has to wean you off."

Until then, I didn't know Sam took medication.

He slept more, late into the afternoon. He broke my owl music box, a memento from my Aunt Karen. He tore pictures in half and ripped Bunny's ear off while saying it was my fault for cheating on him. I knew I was disgusting, but Sam had never said it or showed it before then.

"Get in the car, I'm driving you back to Hudson," he said, speeding, blowing through EZ pass lanes with no EZ Pass.

"Can I have one too?" I asked timidly as he lit a cigarette.

"No," he said in a way that told me not to talk again.

For three hours we sat like that until finally his foot was on the brake. Without putting the car into park, I got out in the pitch-dark driveway. Before I knocked, the dogs barked. One of my parents let me in, but I can't remember who. In the morning we went to the river. My dad putzed around fixing things, my mom and I sat in the sun, reading books until we were interrupted by Aunt Lia and her boyfriend, who idled their pontoon boat near us.

"What are you doing, Ame," my aunt asked.

"Just moved back from Pennsylvania last night," I answered.

"Oh, I didn't even know you went. What the fuck ya come

back here for?" She laughed.

"Because Sam's an asshole," my mom answered for me.

"Well, fuck him," my aunt added, laughing more, instinctively having my back like my mom because they didn't need or want to know the circumstances of my midnight delivery.

"Come hang out at our camp," my aunt offered, knowing what I needed without me having to say so.

My dad's disposition told me he didn't want me to go. Not with them, not with his baby sister who still took pride in things my father left far behind.

"How's she going to get back, you guys won't be able to drive later," my dad said condescendingly.

"Little Lia can sleep over," my aunt's boyfriend laughed, as he called me by the nickname given to me because Aunt Lia and I were the wild ones. She rode a Harley, drank Jack Daniel's, fought men (and won); I had a winning record for school fights and a reputation for suspensions and smoking weed.

Drinking around their fire, Aunt Lia sang Allman Brothers songs and turned the volume all the way up when Pure Prairie League's "Amie" came on, the song she sang to me every time she saw me. With each beer we drank, my problems felt further away.

Until morning came.

Waking up there worsened how heavy the weight of being back was. Alone again, yearning to go to a home that I hadn't found yet.

• • •

Saturday night, I stood in Ivy's driveway leaning against a car, drinking a 40 while two boys from my grade joked, "What, did Sam keep you locked up? Look how pale you are!"

Noticing I was also nauseous, I touched my hand to my breastbone, realizing my chest felt tender too. The feeling washed over me, "I'm pregnant."

Tuesday, the first week of eleventh grade, when school let out, I walked to Planned Parenthood. Sam picked me up, then stayed the night with me in my bedroom—the one that he had delivered me back to a week before. I mostly slept and we barely talked, but in the morning Sam said he loved me and was sorry about the baby.

"Can I come back?" I asked.

"You should stay, finish school," Sam said and left me behind.

But by Friday, he called and said he found us an apartment of our own. "Come home."

In a letter to my parents I wrote, *"I suck at explaining things in person, I can say things much easier by writing, so here it goes. I am only truly happy with Sam, even when we were fighting I still would rather have been there than here. I do like the girls I hang out with, and I have changed (meaning I am not leaving to get away from drugs. I'm past that). I just really love Sam and want to spend the rest of my life with him. So...you're thinking, why can't I wait till after graduation or something. Because the whole reason we were fighting is because when he was gone I would do wrong things so I can't be trusted by him which I completely understand. Things won't work if I can't go now. But I'll finish school and work and only hang out with Sam. I would rather do that than go to stupid parties with the same people and do the same things. I've done that for 3 years, I have to move on but no one here my age or older is past drinking and partying, Sam is. And he forgives me now. If I don't go I know I'll get depressed again, I'm on a different level than people in my grade, I grew up faster than I should have but that's how it is. I have been through so much stuff dealing with boys and drugs and death and just everything. I've had to really think seriously about things before, I've been so depressed at times and learned so much, I'm not just a little 16 year old who wants to run away with her boyfriend. I know this is the right thing to do. Sorry I didn't talk to you about it,*

I'm more comfortable writing. I love you guys and sorry if this hurts you, it's nothing to do with problems with you, I just really need to do this and move on in my life. That honestly won't happen here. Sorry, love ya."

• • •

Unable to attend school in a different state with no legal guardian, I searched the classifieds. Being sixteen, having no diploma and only dishwashing experience, made finding jobs to circle and call challenging.

Hoping my odds would be better on foot, I explored downtown Bethlehem. At the end of the street, I was taken in yet intimidated by a hotel. The windows towered over me. The entrance resembled a drawbridge to a castle with flags soaring above, an American one and two others I didn't recognize. Nervously I asked an attractive lady at the front desk for an application. "I'd be grateful for any position. And I really love cleaning," I told her, wishing this would be the one.

No one called from there, or anywhere I hoped for, which forced me to take the first job offered. In the basement level of a building I had never been to, I walked the musty hallway, feeling lost and afraid. I anxiously opened a door, hoping it was the right one. Inside, an extremely heavy-set woman sat behind a desk placed in the front center of the room. Like a teacher. Instead of students in her view, two rows of divided spaces held drug addicts and work release program participants reading scripts, as I would learn to do too. "Hello, this is Amy from R.A. Haney. I'm giving away a fifty-dollar coupon to Price Rite grocery store in exchange for receiving a FREE estimate for new windows, siding, and home improvements," I said too quietly into a telephone receiver. Feeling inadequate and hating my own voice, I hung up at the first sign of hesitation from the poor person on the other end. My boss yelled, her words always muffled by a mouth full of food, "You have to make them say no three times."

Desperately needing a way out, I tried to go away from wanting to die toward trying harder.

At the library, I created a resume that focused on my new skill set, sales. This led to me being offered a better-paying position at a more reputable telemarketing establishment, selling newspaper subscriptions over the phone. The building was cleaner, the people more normal. I made friends with a skateboarder guy with gauged ears. "I'm going to get out of here, get my GED," he told me while we sat outside smoking.

Back at the library, I looked it up and learned that I could take the test too. When I read that the diploma wouldn't be issued till my eighteenth birthday, I silently worried that I wouldn't make it two more years. Deciding to have a backup plan, in case I was still alive, I signed up for the test.

Bethlehem High School felt foreign but familiar too, like Hudson. Like all schools, lockers lined halls full of doors leading to classrooms. A sign pointed me toward the one I needed. People trickled up to the front returning their finished tests and I wondered why I was so slow, the second to last done.

Monday at work, I asked my friend how he thought he did. "I didn't even finish. Gave it and left," he said. Friday, our boss announced we'd be closing for good. When we clocked out, that was it, the company was closed.

・・・

I borrowed Sam's car during the day because he worked the night shift at a cement plant. Driving to the town over, I held back tears as I navigated the unfamiliar, long stretch of the strip which was packed full of cars turning into various shopping centers. Finally finding the location of my newest job didn't feel better; inside, I hated talking on the phone. Talking at all. At lunch, I didn't dare move the car, instead I cried in it. By the end of the week, I was pulled aside and told I wasn't a good fit, "not quite as high-spirited" as they needed.

Early the next morning, I walked to a small gray building on the corner of a dumpy street and met with a woman who said she could help me find a job more suited for me. Within minutes of her searching the boxy computer in front of her, she said, "There's a dog grooming job just around the block!"

I went straight there and did so every day after because I loved the dogs. The downfall was the family dynamics. Suzanne, the owner, hired her mother to answer the phone out front and greet people too. Suzanne's daughter Jess groomed dogs with us in the back. The three of them sprung into screaming matches, stormed off, and then came back, at least weekly but sometimes daily. When it was Suzanne's fault, she gave us money for lunch at Wawa. When Jess felt bad, she'd take the keys to Suzanne's SUV and fill up the gas tank.

By 2001, after being there almost two years I asked, "Do you think I could have Christmas week off? My eighteenth birthday is on the 27th!"

"You just had a week off over the summer."

"When I had poison ivy?"

"Yes."

"But you said I couldn't come in because I'd give it to the dogs," I said, thinking back to how Sam washed my hair for me that week. How I was unable to get my hands wet because, as Suzanne knew, in addition to my entire body itching, my right pointer, middle, and index fingers were broken, and I had seven stitches sutured in the shape of a check mark on my left palm.

Unable to get the time off and being bad at taking no for an answer, we moved back to Hudson. The move was for me to see my family but also for Sam, who hadn't found his footing or happiness in Pennsylvania.

· · ·

Sam said he'd find work with Frank; instead, they mostly fished. Without asking me first, Sam bought a boat with Frank, using the money I worked hard for at the rat farm.

I woke up at 5 a.m., drove half an hour away, washed my body in a small shower and suited up in a baby-blue polyethylene jumpsuit. I duct-taped my socks and gloves to the blue plastic cuffs so no air could escape. I put on a duck-billed face mask, a helmet over my head and hooked up tubes and breathing apparatuses before heading into a long narrow room, in what was basically a trailer. I cleaned cages which sometimes flooded, finding full families of drowned, dead mice. Or worse, cold and trying to swim. When the mom mouse didn't eat all the pups, I'd have to separate them and punch little holes in their ears to identify who was who. I'd numb their tiny tails before using a straight razor to cut the tip off and send it away to a lab in a labeled vial. I'd ship the mice too, in hard, white plastic containers to colleges and medical facilities all over the world. I knew it was for a good cause, my mice specifically to cure Alzheimer's, but that didn't make it less sad that they were dying.

For my first paid vacation, we went with Frank's family to the Bahamas. The first night I cried alone on the beach. I loved Sam but still felt lost. Toward the end of our trip, Sam got down, one knee in the sand, and proposed.

I said yes.

We talked about buying a house in New York but instead moved to Manteno, Illinois, hoping to find happiness there.

・・・

In Illinois, Sam and I started the spring semester at Kankakee Community College. My major was Small Business Management. I dreamed of opening my own dog grooming salon, adding daycare, boarding, and training too—a combination I hadn't seen yet. Sam's was something I can't remember but he left after the first semester, wanting to move back to Pennsylvania. We agreed I'd stay and finish the summer semester I had already started, while he looked for an apartment.

After class, I rushed to Mike and Melissa's apartment complex. The two of them were sitting outside on the curb with a friend I'd never met before. Neighbors and a news crew surrounded them. One woman told us that a small grill on the balcony below Mike and Melissa's apartment caused the fire. Everything was gone—Melissa's newly bought wedding dress, Mike's art supplies and the paintings he had already made and sold.

We asked around about their cats and found out all three jumped. One seemed to limp, but they all ran off into the woods behind us. The four of us searched and only called it quits when the sun was fully down and we couldn't see anymore. Mike, Melissa, and the guy I didn't know invited me back to the guy's house. He made us vodka, sprite, and something-fruity drinks. I told him how good it tasted. He said it was a concoction he learned bartending at Friday's, which was near Red Lobster, where Mike and I worked. He took me on a tour through his basement, paintings hung like clothes from a line. "You made all these?" I asked.

"I did!"

"What are they?"

"They're inspired by Radiohead."

In his living room, I asked who the girl was in the framed photographs. He said, "An old friend." Mike and Melissa, rightfully tired and distraught, left early.

I stayed for a few more.

I only remember after—the light dimmed from a red cloth he placed over the lamp on the table near his bed. Tapestries decoratively hung on the walls. I on my stomach, he softly caressed my naked back, telling me how beautiful I was, soft. The first to make me feel that way too.

"What music is this?" I asked.

"'Laid,' by James."

In the early morning, I crept through the house, careful not to wake up Sam's parents and brother. Later, I wondered if my cheeks looked like fire as I told the whole truth of what happened, minus the end.

I didn't understand myself.

I loved them.

Sam's mom and I spent endless nights on the front porch together. She always made sure there was cornbread for me. We went to Sam's brother's games. They were my family. Sam was my life. We had been through so much bad, but had great things too—the peace protest on Valentine's Day in New York City, drives to nowhere, cabins and camping...

Finish school. Fix my drinking. Fix myself. Handle it alone, so no one gets hurt, I told myself.

• • •

In Pennsylvania, Sam and I did normal things.

We watched *The Simpsons* and then bought two bunnies and named them after characters in the show too. "Lenny, white. Carl, black." They ran around our living room, chasing our big orange cat, Cody. Finally, we had a nice place, with a pool too.

"Let's go swim," I said to Sam,

"No, it's too hot to swim."

"That doesn't even make sense," I said.

When I'd ask him to go for walks, he'd say no to that too. Sometimes we went to bars, other times Sam sat drinking while I waited tables. The girls I worked with said he seemed like he was sulking and asked, "What are you doing with him? Don't marry him." The guys in the kitchen said it too. For me, I missed Sam's sense of humor. The happier I felt, the more I tried to bring him there with me, the further away he went.

I knew I owed him. Not only for the things he didn't know, but because he helped me leave Hudson.

I didn't deserve to be okay if he wasn't.

• • •

We spent Christmas in New York with my family.

Two days later, on my twenty-first birthday, we arrived in Las Vegas. Sam and I found my sister, who had flown in earlier with her college roommates. We did normal Vegas things, going from casino to casino, stopping at Circus Circus because *Fear and Loathing* was one of my favorite films. On the second night, Sam said he needed nicer shoes for the club; dancing the night away with a Ken doll lookalike, we joked that Sam must have bought dancing shoes. Soon after though, Sam disappeared. A pattern no place was able to break.

The next day, walking to find food, Jamie said, "Is that Sam?" Slouched over at a blackjack table, completely hammered, Sam was spending our savings. We lured him away with pizza before bringing him back to the room. While he slept, I drank in Jamie's room, watching her and her friends switch from sweatpants to dresses. Several times, they asked, "Are you sure you're staying? The limo will be fun, come!"

"Nah. We can't waste backstage passes! We're going to the show. Sam said he just needed to sleep a little."

Alone on the strip, I asked officers for directions. Trying to memorize the names of the roads felt impossible and when one road was blocked off, I felt defeated. Afraid to be lost, I skipped the Moe show and went back and watched Avril Lavigne sing songs and the ball drop on the hotel television while Sam slept.

Happy New Year.

Sam recouped in time for the Stratosphere the next night but was drunk enough that I had to go looking for him again. When I told him I swore I saw him kissing one of the girls we came with, he said it wasn't true and I didn't fight any more about it because I knew I deserved it.

• • •

After smoking a hookah in the attic of Jake's house, we ate hummus and pita around a small table in the kitchen. As I fed scraps to Cleo the German shepherd, I told Jake about Vegas and he told me he thought he was falling for me. "Your life doesn't have to be like that."

• • •

I don't remember telling Sam.

I don't recall any fighting or yelling or anything at all, just that my manager, who became my close friend, let me move into his walk-in closet.

The closet had no door and was located at the end of his hallway. I pushed a mattress up to the wall and hung a thin rope above it, where I attached pictures and art with small wooden clothespins. On the opposite wall, a silver circular rod held half of his clothes and half of mine. I lined my Salvation Army T-shirts up in order of my favorites first. Happy and still in bed, I pulled the *Fiddler on the Roof* one down, admiring that I didn't have to get out of bed to get dressed. I felt at home in my small space.

"The only thing I'm missing is music," I told Jake, who came back a few days later with a CD player.

"Aww. Thank you!"

"Put something on!" he said.

"I don't have anything."

"That's why I got you this too," he smiled, giving me a thick brown leather case that held over fifty CDs he had burned for me.

"This is the sweetest gift anyone has given me."

JAKE WAS LIGHT.
Sweet and seemingly untouched from darkness.

A COUPLE WEEKS into dating, Jake finished teaching me my second poker lesson. We walked at midnight to the gas station for hot chocolate and when we returned, he stood in the kitchen and said, "I'm so in love with you."
Days later, my roommate yelled, "Phone!"
Barely able to understand Sam, I heard him say, "My brother was in a car accident. Come home. We have to go now."
The plane landed. We met Sam's family at the Ronald McDonald Foundation. Their shuttle bus brought us directly to the hospital. Sam's brother's body looked the same: young, strong, and healthy. His head did not. It was so swollen. Perfectly round. Large. Immediately imprinted into my memory forever.

AT SOME POINT, we left the hospital.
Back at the Ronald McDonald House, we tried to sleep but morning came fast. Walking the hospital halls, I whispered to Sam, "What are those marks on everyone's head?"
"Ash Wednesday."
Sam's parents asked if I wanted a moment alone to say goodbye. "He loved you like a sister."
I loved him like the little brother he was.
When I lived with Sam's family, I took him to get fast food and to rent movies. He let me do Tae Bo workout videos in his bedroom. We played basketball on his trampoline, and all hung out in the kitchen after school, talking. He was sweet. At sixteen he wasn't drinking or partying, he was playing sports. The star pitcher. Almost guaranteed to follow in his favorite

player Derek Jeter's footsteps.

• • •

A teenage boy stood in the bed of a truck. His radio played Sarah McLachlan to the kids in the field, who created a memorial for their classmate and friend. Sam's sister's knees buckled instantly to the sound and sight of it. I got down on the ground with her and rubbed her back as she let out the deepest, most sorrowful cries I'd ever heard.

Turning the ignition, "Tears in Heaven" played. The absurdity of it being on before the funeral made us all laugh. The service itself did not. Little #2 and Derek Jeter pins plastered everywhere.

Lying in the bedroom that Sam and I once shared in Illinois, I heard laughter below from the living room. A homemade movie played; people told stories as should be done; all I could think was that I wished I could take the pain away from the family. For some reason, I felt built to carry it, as if I were made to do so. But I failed to help where they really needed me. "You have to go get him, you're the only one," Sam's mom said to me when he disappeared to the bar. I wished I could; I tried to pry him away but we both knew it couldn't be me anymore.

"Amy, you'll get a ride back to Hudson with Uncle Dan, we'll meet you back there," Sam's sister told me. At a rest stop in a state I don't remember, a middle-aged woman wore a skirt made of black lace, decorated with red hearts. She looked ridiculous as she nicely said to me, "Happy Valentine's Day." I hated her.

Sleeping as much of the ride as I could, we got back and prepared for another set of memorials in New York.

• • •

Short and cold, February wasn't done with me.

It was confirmed that the body found in November was Joey, my cousin.

At Bates and Anderson Funeral Home, our family gathered around poster boards full of his pictures and finally accepted he was no longer missing.

• • •

I read passages from *The Giver*, explaining snow, sledding, and the red of an apple to Nanu, my grandmother, at Columbia Memorial Hospital just before she died.

"I can't do another funeral, I'm sorry," I told my mother.

"It's okay, go," she said.

• • •

In Pennsylvania, Sam wondered if these tragedies would bring us back together. As much as I wanted love to be the answer, wanted Sam to be, I couldn't go back. For that, I knew I was a bad person. I owed him. But in the seven years together, we never figured out how to heal ourselves. I needed to keep trying, moving. Or I'd never make it, I thought.

• • •

"My grandma has a condo in Florida, we could go," Jake offered, trying to save me.

I let him try.

Like I let Sam.

Aunt Karen

Left to right: Hopper and her mom, me and my mom,
Aunt Karen, Jamie and Poppy (grandfather)

May I Have This Dance.....

I saw as a picture revealed unto me
It floated and moved 'round my head
As clear as a bell I saw them
Not a word was spoken or said.

The Man was dressed in whitest of whites
Bearded face and sandals of tan
Scarred hands and scarred feet...His glory
He was Jesus....The Son of Man

And, she was tired and hurting
A bed of affliction so long
Our sister in Christ, our Karen,
Was waiting till He played their song.

Then Heaven responded with music
None ever was heard on this Earth.
It's played for His bride who loves Him,
It's saved for their wondrous new birth.

And The Man dressed in white was smiling,
As He stopped lending breath to His bride
He reached down and took her tiny small hand,
And brought her to stand by His side.

His eyes were happy and smiling,
His look much more than a glance.
With love in His voice, He asked her,
"Dear Karen, may I have this dance?"

She placed her small hand on His shoulder,
'Round her waist He placed His scarred hand,
They waltzed together on streets of gold,
As angels played harps from their band.

Our Karen was smiling a radiant smile,
As I watched her dance with The King.
She giggled and laughed while waltzing,
....And, I know I heard her sing.

I saw them dance till both out of sight.
The Bridegroom had claimed His sweet bride.
Her faith in her Jesus rewarded,
Forever she'll be by His side.

When we get to Heaven, I'm certain
There's no guessing and never per chance,
Karen will still be waltzing,
....Our Jesus has asked her to dance.

Jill Owens
February, 1996

Poem that was read during my Aunt Karen's wake

Mom and Dad (Cover)

Jamie and me

Left to right: Kaia, Jamie, and me. Bunks in our cabin on the Hudson River

Hopper and I on the Hudson River

Joey and his mom, Maryann

Joey and his dad, Joe. Our camp, on the Hudson River

Joey and me

Joey

Mom + Dad
I am so sorry. You were wonderful parents and did absolutely nothing wrong. I've never, not for one second doubted my love for you. I love you. I am sorry for always hurting you and dissappointing you. I know you loved me to though. So never question our love for eachother. There was nothing you could do for me. I just couldn't live with myself anymore. I wasen't strong enough. I gave up and I am so sorry because I know how much this is going

to hurt you. I'm selfish too. I'm sorry. I just couldn't feel like this anymore. I love you.
Amy

Jamie,
 I know what I just did will affect you for the rest of your life and I am so sorry. I hope you will some day forgive me. I loved you more then any one else in the world. We had a great relationship and there was nothing I would have changed with you. I love you with all my ♡. There was nothing you could have done for me either though. There was nothing anyone could have done

> I couldn't deal with *me* anymore. I don't like the type of person I was. I know I'm being selfish and I haven't did this so many times only for the fact I didn't want to hurt you or anyone else but I just can't do it anymore. I can't feel like this and I have no other options. Please don't let anyone read my journal, except maybe Sam. Tell Sam I love him and I'm sorry!
> Amy

Suicide Notes. Written when I was 15

Me and Broadus

PART THREE

Back to Circa 2016

"After all, we are nothing more or less than we choose to reveal."

SYLVIA PLATH

Broken Gut

Searching for the thing that would save my marriage and myself, I filled my journal with pro and con lists: Go back to the Department of Social Services vs. run a café.

"It's in the developmental stage. We're open to ideas," the hipster couple from the café said, only communicating through text messages.

"Great! Should we meet in person?" I eventually asked.

Walking on Warren Street en route to them, I passed Bystro and thought, *Their money probably comes from David.* David was the father of the hipster husband and owned Bystro. I knew this because David dated Alexander's sister. Had Alexander chosen differently, he would be celebrating his two-year anniversary as manager of Bystro. In that reality, I'd be meeting Alex for advice. We'd smoke out back, talking about menus and life. After I accepted the position, we'd walk dogs and strollers full of babies when our shifts ended.

If he just made it through February, I thought, for not the first time.

Spring may have saved him.

Grabbing a glimpse of it myself, I let the warm winter sun soak into my skin for a moment before entering the storefront. Inside, glass windows held the heat and rays kissed a collection of old wooden chaise lounge chairs covered with down cushions. Cozy and inviting enough that a non-book-lover would sink into them, resting, reading the day away too.

"Hi, Amy?"

"Yes! Hi. I'm so happy to meet you guys."

"We're a little short on time. We're getting our son from the bus soon."

As I shook the husband's extended hand, I thought how strange it was that they BOTH had to go to the bus stop. As I followed them through the wide, deep antique store, he pointed toward the left side. "That's where we'd make the daycare. Section it off, build wooden boats and structures for kids to climb while their parents shopped and ate."

"Oh, cool."

"Yeah, we'd partner with other places too. Moms getting a massage at Bohdi or shopping in town could use our daycare too."

Further in, past the life-sized horse sculpture and canvases, we reached the back of the building. A coat closet–sized space held an old dishwashing machine. "This is where we'll set up the tiny kitchen for you. We'd build a long counter, you'd take the orders then prepare and serve it, all right here!" he said, excited.

"I would take the order and cook too?"

"Maybe at first. It'd be easy food, Asian infused. Create your own veggie bowl type stuff. We could do little bowls for the kids too!"

"Lunch and dinner?"

"Midday, 10 to 7 or so. Probably six days a week to start off but we'd tweak it depending on how things went business wise."

Talking with Zak, I explained they were nice but weird, and I worried they didn't know what they were doing. Zak assured me he'd help create a menu I could handle.

In my notebook I weighed out the potential for fun, the excitement of being back in the restaurant world, and the possibility of having a day off with Zak against my real reservation—my ability to pull it all off with no experience behind a line.

• • •

The Department of Social Services tried to lessen my fear of being a slave to a clock with fake freedoms—home by 4, weekends and holidays off. The problem was, though, these times didn't suit my situation with Zak. I'd be alone again.

Ultimately, it was all overridden by reading back through my journal on what I lacked from my three days at the bakery. I wanted work with variation. I needed work where it felt like I was helping.

Adult Protective Services offered that with the population it served: homeless, elderly, disabled, and mentally ill clients. More so though, I knew going back to a county job meant downtime, something I hated in the past but planned to use for writing. Writing at work felt warranted because it was how I hoped to help the most people, and it would fix the problem of time feeling wasted.

• • •

"I'm going back in May," I told Jamie.
"Let's do a sister trip first!"
"Okay!"
"I'm running a race in Texas. We'll make Mom go for her sixtieth!" Jamie said.
"She's not going on a plane!"
"She might for Chip and Joanna Gaines," Jamie laughed.
"I'm only going if we can swim in cool swimming holes!"
"We can! In Austin. We'll go there first! It'll make Waco worth it!"

ZAK'S PURSUIT OF acting halted but he still hadn't gone back to cooking, which made it so he could get coverage for his bar shifts. Arriving all together in Austin, we walked to the capitol building and around town. Upstairs at Caroline's seemed fun, but once we were on the Astroturf rooftop with crowds of college-aged kids playing corn hole, we knew we were too old to be there.

For dinner we went to Coopers. The best barbecue in Austin. Suggested to us by Zak's southern chef friend.

The next morning, my mom, Jamie, and I woke up early and walked the trails by the water before going to Wanderlust Yoga for acai bowls. I fell in love with the vibe and idea of owning something so positive and encompassing of mind and body. Zak messaged me, "I'm awake, where are you guys?"

"Across the street, sitting outside. Come?!"

He sat, I offered him bites of my food.

"No, I can't eat yet. I just woke up."

"You should go inside!"

"Nah. I don't want anything. I'm good."

"Yeah, but you should go in because this is what we should open at home! Hudson doesn't have anything like it! We could add healthy salads and stuff too."

Looking around for a second just to please me, we left and loaded the car, where Zak whispered to me, "I'm kinda hungry now."

"We can stop somewhere quick," I said.

"Let's go to that place Jimi worked at."

"There's not enough time for that, plus we all just ate."

"Amy, I told Jimi I'd go there."

"You don't even like Jimi, who cares," I said.

"Amy. Please, c'mon."

Some of the streets were shut off for a street festival, so we walked to where Jimi used to work, thinking it might be faster. The restaurant was further out, but no one was there so we got right in. "Is the food good?" I asked Zak.

"It's only okay."

In the backseat together, Zak whispered again, "Are you mad?"

"I told you we wouldn't have time for both."

"I didn't know we had to be in Waco by a certain time," he said.

"You did. Jamie has to register for the race."

"I'm sorry," he said.

"That's why we each got to pick one thing. You had Coopers."

"Sorry."

"Now we don't get to go to a swimming hole. It's just like what you did in Mexico."

Zak slept in again the next morning while my mom and I walked to the points on the map Jamie marked out. Running past us, Jamie waved as I tried to snap pictures, hoping to capture her coming one step closer toward her goal of checking off a half marathon in each state.

After the race, Zak joined us for shopping at Magnolia's, something that he and I weren't into but was my mom's choice for the trip.

On the last day we swam and read by the pool. Zak cooked us a nice dinner on the outdoor grill. Jamie and my mom went to bed by dark, while Zak and I committed ourselves to finishing a bottle of vodka we bought, knowing we couldn't bring it on the plane in the morning. Sitting at the metal patio table, Zak showed me the new video for "This is America," which we watched at least five times. Not once did I ask him to get off his phone, because he was including me. The conversation flowed effortlessly; it wasn't forced. I didn't have to ask him to talk to me. It felt different. Better.

・・・

For as long as I could remember, I was the first one in the water; even as an adult, people called me "Mermaid." I loved doing laps and after, to relax, I'd release the air from my lungs and sink softly to the bottom. I'd stare up at the sun shooting silver specks through the water, wondering if dying felt that way too. Always the last one out of the water too, I wished my hair would stay wet forever, which was why when Zak said he wanted to get into fishing, I was happy to have a hobby to share.

I used my paddles, which read "Day Tripper." They were given to me by my mother to accompany the red kayak she found for me at a yard sale, over a decade ago. Worn and unwavering, it was invaluable; the vessel that produced a friendship between my mom and me, after Florida.

Zak used the hunter-green kayak I bought, a sit on top type. It had two holes to hold fishing poles while nooks made room for coolers and tackle. He folded his bandana long and thin and tied it around his forehead. He wore swimming shorts with pineapples or stripes, paired with tank tops and his light fishing flannel, keeping him warm when the sun wasn't out. He was adorable.

He signed up for a monthly subscription box that brought new hooks, weights, rubber worms, and stickers that I plastered on potted plants inside and outside our house. Fish playing the banjo, fish dressed up as women, fish reading a book and one fish that wore a hat and sat in a boat, catching a man with ginger-colored hair with a sandwich on his hook.

Before the water was warm enough to swim in, Zak and Isaac met on the lake before sunrise, whenever they could. Sometimes it secretly annoyed me, but I never wanted to be the wife who said, "Why didn't you ever wake up early with me to do stuff," so instead, I chose to be hopeful we'd be like that on our future days off too. This made it easier to shove any bitterness over our lost time away and be genuinely happy for him to have something he loved, until the line between hobby and obsession became quickly blurred.

"Where are you?" I texted.

"Still on the water, headed to shore soon."

"Jamie's here, I thought you wanted to come to dinner with us? Should we wait?"

"Yes, I want to come! I never get to!"

Time passed.

We waited. "Where are you?"

No reply.

Then finally, "My shorts were wet. I didn't want to get in the truck like that."

"That doesn't even make sense..." I wrote.

My truck was old. A reliable workhorse. Carting kayaks; carrying dirt, stone, and furniture for me and friends. No one would ever need to dry off, for hours, before getting in. At a 9 p.m. dinner with Jamie, I didn't have to explain. She knew. If it wasn't fishing, it was fights, magic, video games, or a newfound love for football, for one season. Mostly it was his phone he drowned me out with.

• • •

Following my Saturday routine, as soon as my eyes opened and I was out of bed, I worked out, cleaned the house and then watered the plants. By noon I sent text messages, hoping someone would want to swim in a pool, go on the river, or drink outside, anywhere in the summer sun. Waiting for responses, I pulled the hammock that hung on a metal frame away from our only tree. I took off my shirt, my sports bra still sweaty; I tucked my tiny shorts tight, exposing as much skin as I could without changing into a bikini. Holding *Legs Get Led Astray* at the perfect altitude, I created enough shade to read the words on the page while my body absorbed as much sun as it could. Halfway through the book, my phone vibrated. "Come to the Rod and Gun Club," my cousin wrote.

Alone too much of the day, my thoughts went to the in-between place they always did, where I both wanted people and felt it was too late because my mood already changed; I worried I wouldn't be fun. The talkative version of me who made people laugh felt out of reach; quieter now, I felt too weird to be near anyone. I kept reading.

"It's the family picnic!" he wrote.

Horseshoe tournaments sounded fun.

"Get here. I'm drinking all the Jack!" he wrote.

I shouldn't drink. I shouldn't go, I thought.

"You have to come!"

Why am I being weird, I grew up there, I thought. One of my earliest memories was there, and those were rare. Hazy, but I had it: A girl, older than Jamie, with fire-red hair smoking in the bathroom, where I followed her in, like a puppy. She was a half-sister. I wasn't sure what that meant but I wanted one, or to be hers. She lifted me to the small and narrow window, I think because the lock on the door was broken, and we were stuck inside. I don't remember if I went through it or how we left the bathroom.

"I'm leaving soon, you have to come!" my cousin said.

He was right. If I didn't see him and something happened in Iraq or Afghanistan, I'd never forgive myself.

Under the pavilion, folding tables formed in the shape of a U held tin trays full of macaroni and cheese, pasta salads, and deviled eggs. Pots held pepperoni and meatballs. Big burly men cooked hot dogs and hamburgers on the grill. It was the same as every birthday and graduation party there. Weddings, funerals, and the family picnics too. It was Stottville. My home.

Standing with my cousin, his mother came over and said, "Stan's girlfriend just hit your truck."

"What?!"

"She was going to drive away! I told her she better not."

A few of us walked up to the parking lot together. "You guys have insurance, right?" I asked.

"Yeah, I'll call you this week, we'll figure it out," Stan promised.

Hours later, when I should've gone home, I said, "I'll drive us there."

"Holy shit, your back door doesn't open! You better make sure Stan pays you," an old friend said.

WE ARRIVED AT the inground pool, lit up with little lights. Taking off my shirt and shorts, I joined the handful of others swimming in their underwear. Being weightless and liberated in water was taken away when my old friend attempted to kiss me. Pulling away, I said, "Sorry."

"No, I'm so sorry. I'm embarrassed," he said.

"Really, it's okay. Don't be embarrassed."

"It's the whisky and nostalgia," he said.

I believed him but was still sad it took me so many times to learn the same lesson: boys never wanted to be my friend.

. . .

While Zak slept, I went to fill the truck with gas but that was too dented to open too.

"Dad, can I use a Debrino truck?"

"What's wrong with yours?"

"Stan hit it yesterday, I'll leave it at the shop so you can see."

"Take the white one you always use," he said.

Climbing in, the cracked leather seats were hot. The floor mats covered in small stones held empty Pepsi and Newport containers. Fidgeting with the air conditioning, I decided it must not work and rolled the windows down, while cranking Radio Woodstock up. Before Shakedown Street ended, I was back in my driveway.

I packed our small cooler with hard seltzers and IPAs; loaded my bag with a book to read and one to draw in. Carefully, I chose what charcoal, graphite, and erasers to place in the cute woodland creatures carrying case Zak bought me. Out back, I dragged one kayak out at a time, hurling them into the bed of the truck. With everything piled in, I went back inside and gently kissed Zak's forehead. "Everything's ready to go!"

Slowly, he was ready and into the truck.

Noticing he was more than his usual level of grumpiness, I said, "What is it, just say it."

"Nothing."

"Just say it. Why are you so mad?"

"The truck."

"It's fine," I said.

"It's not fine, Amy."

"It's really not a big deal. We have this one to use. We're still going to the lake. It doesn't have to ruin our day."

"You're always like, 'It's not a big deal,' but it is."

"It's not. Stan will pay to get it fixed, and it's my truck. I don't know why you care so much."

"I just don't understand why you had to go there. You know stuff like that happens with people like that."

"People like what?"

"You know, Amy."

"Like my family? Sorry my family isn't good enough for you."

"That's not what I meant."

It was, but I let it go so we wouldn't waste a day.

Zak fished while I tried to read *The Voice of Knowledge* by Don Miguel Ruiz, but it only annoyed me that day.

"Wanna take a break? Explore the lake with me?"

"Sure!" Zak said, except he continued to cast, stopping so long that when I looked back, he was barely visible.

Going back to where he was, I told him, "I'll meet up with you later."

Paddling toward land, I stopped and drew the distant hills until that became tiresome too.

"Let's swim!" I said to Zak when I found him again.

"I don't want to."

"Really? Just for a little bit!"

"Amy, c'mon, I don't want to."

More than our boats separated us.

• • •

"That's the guy Pip dated," Whitney said about the guy who sat three stools down from her at Gov's.

"Oh yeah, I saw the pictures she always posted with him." They took selfies in sunglasses, ones with black-and-white filters and some sitting in his green VW bus. Pip's wavy dirty-blonde hair always fell perfectly past her breasts. Her lips were full, eyes blue. She was stunning. Together, they were as beautiful as the scenery.

"Yeah, we were talking about you! We know you from Pip's pictures!" Whitney said to Dillon when he noticed us looking at him; we laughed it off and chatted briefly.

• • •

The second time I saw Dillon was similar.

Same bar.

With Whitney.

This time though, Dillon was with his best friend, Walt.

Walt wasn't my supervisor when I worked in Children's Services, but he was smarter and better at his job than mine was, so when I could, I went to him. Plus, he was a wise ass, which I greatly appreciated. Catching up on our new careers, I noticed Walt and I accidentally spoke in acronyms that no one else understood. To be more inclusive, I switched subjects. "I always wanted a VW bus!"

"I rebuilt it in Hawaii," Dillon said.

"You did! I love Hawaii, I got married there!"

"You did! I lived with my ex and daughters there!"

"Did you love it?"

"I did, we had a chair lift to our house, and I built zip lines in the ocean!"

"What! That sounds amazing! Why would you leave that?"

"I missed the seasons."

"Yeah, I felt like that in Florida too. I think Hawaii would be different for me though. Hiking and swimming are my favorite things!"

"Move there. Try it!"

"I did tell my husband we should!"

"Why didn't you go?"

"At first because I couldn't put my dog on a plane or quarantine him. I'm not sure why we didn't go after he died though. Never too late, I guess!"

Dillon showed me pictures of him and his dog, who died too. They were near fire and water, traveling across the county, from California to New York. He played me videos of his adventures, making Death Proof coffee, and drinking it in delightful places. Literally living my dream.

Multiple IPAs later, and wanting a whisky nightcap, Dillon asked, "Should we go to Wunder?"

"Yes!" we all agreed.

Sitting there together, Walt asked, "Whit, didn't you drive your car into that pond after leaving here?"

"In her defense, we were roofied," I said, laughing.

"That's fucking terrible," Walt said.

"It happens!"

"What! No, it doesn't!" Walt laughed.

"I've been three times," I said before sharing the North Carolina story. "They were like, damn this bitch is like a horse, she won't go down."

Punchline.

Laughs all around.

. . .

In my journal I wrote, *"He gives off a LIVING vibe I love."*

Showering, I imagined us drinking coffee in the morning, whisky at night, both by firelight. Adventures in between. Swimming in waterfalls, hiking mountainsides. I touched myself at the thought of us together, in his bus or on a blanket under the stars, surrounded only by evergreen trees. Making love.

Afterwards, I thought, *It's not him I like. It's the life I'm drawn to. Maybe Zak and I could have that still.*

. . .

"You should come out with us! Meet Dillon," I told Elle.

"Oh, that's the guy who's always in Pip's pictures!"

"Yeah," I laughed, telling her how Whitney and I were caught at the bar for that.

"He's always somewhere so dreamy," Elle said.

"I know! Like, I want that life!"

"Right?! How do we be like Dreamy Dillon," Elle said.

I laughed, and we both continued to refer to him as Dreamy Dillon after that night.

. . .

Walt, Dillon, and I sat at Gov's. Elle arrived last. As she wildly explained how hard it was to leave the house because of the kids, I watched her presence steal the room. For me, she was the most beautiful and I loved that her gestures were somehow both muted and animated. Her hands moved while she spoke, then they were searching through her oversized bag, pulling out a box of Uno cards. We played a game that went on for far too long, but finally stopped when Sean stumbled in.

"Zakkkk!" Sean said, drunk.

"That's not Zak, it's Dillon." I laughed and added, "We could go to Helsinki and see him though! He's almost done."

"Yes! It's been so long," Elle agreed.

Bubbly and light, we all walked the few blocks to get there. Inside, still behind the bar, Zak looked so sexy in his vest and tie. Eight years later, I was still stunned by him. "Come with us for one?" I asked.

"I'm gonna finish up here and go home."

"Just one. Please," I whispered while the group talked.

"Amy, I'm tired. I don't want to go out."

"I know, but just one. Elle never gets a babysitter."

"Amy, no. C'mon."

The next morning, I wrote about how Zak was wrapped up in his world of weed and video games. I said I wanted to believe he was okay, but I wondered if he was depressed too, dealing with it in his own way.

• • •

Drinking red wine, Elle and I sat on the rug in her living room. "Dillon and I texted some but there wasn't really a connection."

A few nights later, in the same seats on her floor, Elle said, "I saw Dillon at the gym, he didn't even say hi! So awkward and weird!"

"So weird," I agreed.

He became "Not so dreamy Dillon" after that.

• • •

I wore a thin tank top, pale pink, almost white. A thick blue stripe through the center. Under it a thin, light sports bra. On the bottom, my favorite CrossFit shorts, small and black with underwear built in, given to me by Whitney. My Army-green rain boots were ankle high and had orange laces. My hair was slightly wavy from air drying and the dampness from the day. On a side road covered with dirt, we passed cows that grazed on fields of green grass as the sun started to peek out. Inside the brewery, built to keep the farm financially afloat, Kaia, Phil, and I danced some while Whitney and Maggie stood, sipping beers.

"Weird, he's everywhere now!" I whispered to Whitney when I saw Dillon walking in, toward us.

"Hey," he said.

"Hi! I didn't know you'd be here," I said.

"Phil mentioned you guys might come."

"I didn't even know you were friends with Phil!"

"I play guitar in the band with them!"

"What! How did I not know that?"

Phil was Stottville's paperboy before I could really remember, making me question if my first recollection of him was my own or borrowed from stories passed down by neighborhood kids. Legend had it that Max, my aunt's German shepherd, bit Phil on the butt before he could pedal away on his BMX bike. Later, I remembered Kaia dating him. They were around sixteen. I was maybe ten. By the time I reached fourteen, I walked to their house next to the Stottville VFW and knocked on the door, asking for acid. They nicely told me to leave. When I moved away, I made sure to go to their annual Christmas party every year. I came back for their wiccan wedding, where we jumped over a broom stick and broke bread together. Throughout our lives we had fires for camping and random parties too, always yelling, "STOTTVILLE!" At Bonnaroo, a music festival in Manchester, Tennessee, Phil even managed to make the whole crowd shout, "STOTTVILLE." Phil made my heart happy when he told people I was like a sister to him. Validating a history in my head—Stottville meant something, which meant people meant something too, not only to me.

Moving to the groove of Grateful Dead songs, the band announced it was time to take a break. The quiet left space to speak. Dillon stood next to me.

"I was thinking of getting into photography," I told him.

"You should!" he said.

"What camera do you use? All your pictures are so good!"

"Just the iPhone 10! I'll show you," he said.

Leaning in toward me he took some shots as I said, "I hate having my picture taken!"

"They'll be so good!"

"I'm zero photogenic! So is my sister. I think it's genetic!"

"I'll prove it! I'll send you some!"

"Tennessee Whisky" poured out of the barn, filling the summer night with the sweet sound only certain songs could provide.

"You have to go?" he asked.

"I do. I'm not the driver!"

"Ask them to meet somewhere for one more?" Dillon said.

"Wish I could."

• • •

With the normal amount of my morning after drinking dread, I journaled, "*Days and pages just pass by and it blows my mind that I have been struggling with alcohol for twenty years. With the same problems for 20 years.*

I need to change.

But also, I had fun last night, dancing, talking.

Connecting."

By nightfall, Dillon sent me black-and-white photographs.

I couldn't stop looking at them.

At us.

At the way I looked at him.

He clearly captured a feeling I didn't yet admit to myself I had.

• • •

"Are you not washing your hair after you swim in pools?" The man who didn't normally cut my hair asked.

"No," I admitted.

"You should, the chlorine really damages it!"

"Yeah, I'll never do that! I swim so much! Then go home and go to bed!"

"At least spray it with a conditioner when you get out!"

The following day, I dolloped drops of Pantene Pro-V in a small, pasture-green-colored spray bottle I had on hand for misting my plants. After filling the rest with water, I placed the nozzle back on and wrapped thin, black hair ties around it for the future. Fitting it perfectly into my bookbag's side pocket, I was happy to create more room for beers and my book on the inside. My towel was twisted and wrapped around my handlebars, earbuds in my ears, as I rode my bike to my aunts.

Besides the barking from the dogs, my early-afternoon swim was quiet. Drinks gone, I shoved my book back into my bag and took out my phone.

"I'm at Wunder, come say hi," a text message said.

Unsure how to answer, I stayed on the deck, laying in the sun until my swimsuit was dry, wondering if it would be weird, just the two of us. *What would we talk about,* I thought.

Spraying my unwashed hair with my new concoction, I tied my tangled strands into some strange bun and pulled my shirt and shorts on. Sitting on the seat of my bike, trying to decide to go home or not, I wrote back.

"Still at Wunder?"

"Yes, come!"

"Okay! A ride into town does sound fun, plus I'm starving," I said, promising myself with no lights on my bike, I'd be home before sunset.

Dillon sat at the first stool in sight. He drank a tall Tito's with club soda. I ordered the same, only adding an orange instead of lemon. Time passed invisibly, eaten up by the fever and loveliness of learning to know a new person with whom laughter and conversation fell so easily.

The pattern of different pacing left one of us always finishing first. "One more," we'd alternatingly say to Safia, the bartender. At least once I said, "I shouldn't. I have to go home."

Still not willing to surrender to the night, after Wunder had closed we stood outside smoking with Safia and Cash, her husband. In his southern accent, Cash said, "You can't ride that thing home."

"I'm fine, I swear."

"No, you're not. I'll drive you home. Put your bike in my truck."

BEFORE ZAK LEFT for work, I was normally up and out of bed. When I wasn't, he asked, "You okay, love?"

"No. I have to quit drinking," I said.

Never needing to know my motivation, he kissed me sweetly on my forehead and left for work. Foggy details drove me out of bed and to the backyard.

Fuck, I thought when my bike wasn't there.

Wanting to wash it all away, I stripped my clothes off and stared at my naked body in the bathroom mirror. Scrapes ran down my back. Physical proof of what I was. Of what I remembered...

Dillon stopped in the road. He didn't pull into our driveway.

Before that though, we kissed softly. Yet fiercely. Against a brick wall, but I don't remember which one or where. Then more, pressed against his truck before we climbed in. Before he delivered me home to my husband.

The pillow still wet from my hair, I reached for my journal. *"I hated your cowboy-ish boots with the buckle. I don't know if I hate or love your shell necklace. I think I like it despite how much I dislike people trying too hard to be something. What are you trying to be?*

I don't know if I feel those things I just wrote.

Am I trying to convince myself I don't like you?

That I regret you?

That sometimes I live too hard in the moment and that's not good?

I don't have to sink into my mistake, be swallowed up by you. Or is it too late? Am I already?

I feel crazy right now. My heart might beat out of my chest, yet I feel numb.

I love Zak.

I asked again if we could move. Do a 'couples' job, run a resort or something together. Live on a beach for a few years. I just want time. Time together. I have been asking for that since the first year. Should/can I be a good sober wife and we start over?

Or is it too late for that?

Maybe.

Probably.

I am not the worst, but I am not good. I suck. My fuck ups are the unforgivable kind.

Why am I staying married? Out of love? To protect Zak's feelings? Or my own? Am I being cautious, not brave?

Why?

Because I'm scared of depression. Scared to cry every day again. Scared to want to die.

I don't want to die.

I want to live life hard.

I feel legit crazy.

'The voice in our head doesn't belong to us,' A comforting notion when my voice told me to kill myself…But now, now how do I trust myself? Chicken. Egg. Again. Drinking because I'm depressed. Depressed because I'm drinking. I'm not a slut, I'm an alcoholic. Or both. Or neither. I don't know what is true, which means I cannot be true to others. I don't know what feelings to follow because my gut instinct is broken.

Truths:

I have to change this time.

The change 'drink less' isn't working.

I want a soul mate.

How can I believe in a soul mate if I don't believe in a God?

Is my love for nature good enough to serve as God?

Does nothing matter, or everything?"

• • •

Later in the day, Dillon messaged me poetically vague statements. He wasn't sorry or upset, he was broken from Pip and in no place to be anything to anyone. I placed my blame on the vodka and we both vowed it could never happen again. Deleting his phone number, I found Safia on Facebook and asked if she had my bike.

"Yeah, we live on Union," Safia said.

Union was only one street over from Wunder but somehow I was unable to find her apartment. I wanted to write her back, "Leave it outside." On the curb. Like trash. For a trash person. Instead, I said, "Hey, what door are you?"

Safia stepped outside and waved me over. Walking toward her, pure panic poured over me at the thought of talking out loud. My pulse quickened with the type of anxiety that manifested after blacking out. I hoped Dillon and I were alone when it happened. Being drunk in front of her, while embarrassing, was at least a norm for our bartender/patron relationship, cheating was not.

Inside their foyer made of glass and full of wedding flowers, the smell of hydrangeas danced on sunbeams that surrounded my bike. I wanted to die and go home, but we joked about the night before as she insisted I come inside quickly. The living room was bright, the hardwood floors were beautiful. Cash sat on the couch smoking. "I tried to give you a ride home, but that guy you were with was being a dick."

"We were both just drunk," I said.

Defending him, or me.

Us.

"Safia was like, 'Babe, she's a grown woman, let her go.' So I did," Cash said.

We laughed, my stomach twisted, wishing he hadn't listened to his wife. That he stopped me from being me.

"You know though, any guy who puts his hands down your

pants in public isn't good."

They knew.

More than I did.

I hated myself for never following my rules. For not going home before sunset. For not learning that besides Lucas, no boy only wanted friendship from me. For being stupid enough to think I only wanted that from Dillon.

Truth or Die

Dillon and I had a million written goodbyes. None stuck for more than a day. In person, we found ways to orchestrate drinks with mutual friends, never alone. Careful to keep the façade to ourselves and others—we were only friends.

. . .

Walking into Gov's, Walt hugged me hello and said, "Dillon's almost here. He stopped home to switch the truck for the bus."

"Yeah, he mentioned he might come," I responded, thinking how Dillon didn't mention the bus part to me.

Even though they both knew, Walt was the one who eventually asked if I was okay. I explained I was; I was mostly just sad for my dad, I said before quickly explaining that our family agreed my grandmother would be at peace now because no one wants to live in a nursing home, lost in Alzheimer's. "It was so sad when she'd ask for my grandfather or her best friend, like how many times should we tell her they're all dead. I feel like no one even told her when my aunt just died, what's the point."

"True," Walt said.

"The best part is, this was like the third family fight in a row my Aunt Lia started. She's probably banned from Bates and Anderson Funeral Home!"

We laughed, as intended.

Quietly inside me though, the specifics swirled. Aunt Lia's accusations of rape and other hateful words that were thrown through the air, falling heavily onto my grandmother's closed casket, dividing siblings into separate sides of the debate. Deliberately left out from the story too was the part in the parking lot after the cemetery—Jamie and I, both in knee-length black dresses and heels, walking a few steps in front of Zak, who asked, "What are those?"

"What?" I asked.

"On your leg," Zak said, pointing toward my right calf where I found three finger-shaped bruises.

"I don't know."

"From Dillon?"

My heart beat fast. Not because the mystery marks were actually from Dillon. They were not. It raced because unlike the never-mentioned scrapes on my back, it was the first time Zak tore through our silent protective shield, revealing he knew something was wrong with us too. "Why would you say that? Especially right now," I said.

At Gov's, my purposefully omitted unfunny parts of the story allowed Walt, Dillon, and me to move late into the night with ease, weaving lighthearted banter, laughter, and whisky together until Walt finally said he had to leave; had to see his boys before bed. Dillon and I agreed, "Just one more."

Outside of the bar, two parking spaces from each other, Dillon asked, "Wanna check out the bus?"

"Sure!"

He kissed me. First standing. Then on the bed, me on my back, him on top of me. Stopped only by too much alcohol.

In the morning, I wondered if Dillon brought the bus intentionally. If he had motives and what they were. I asked myself the same thing, wondering if we matched—if we were both stupid and staying for one more out of habit or if deep down in our subconscious it was deliberate on both ends. I needed to know what Dillon wanted from me, so I asked, "Should we go on a sober walk in the woods to talk?"

Stepping out of his white truck, he wore weird little hiking sandals and pants made of a strange material, maybe water resistant, even though it was sunny. I thought how Zak would never wear that. How if anyone else did, besides Dillon, I wouldn't like it.

Dillon stayed mostly a few steps behind me as my new dog Lando led us through the narrow trail. As we walked, Dillon spoke about dropping out of high school, getting his GED, and searching for the intangible in relationships and drugs.

"Are we the same person?!" I joked.

Past Beauty Falls and more than halfway through the trail, I said what I hadn't known I came for, "I think I have to tell on myself."

"Yeah?"

"Yes. Sorry."

"Don't be sorry."

"You won't be mad?"

"Of course not. I want you to be happy."

"Ugh. Sorry. You probably think I'm the worst."

"Never. I just don't want you to do it for me. I can't give you what you want."

"I don't want anything. I just can't keep being a liar," I said, meaning it wholeheartedly, not needing him to be more than what he was.

Nearing the end of the loop, Dillon broke our silence and explained he hadn't healed all the way from Pip; he worried her frozen heart bled into his.

"Like I said, I'm just not in a place to be anything to anyone because of her yet. We just have to slow down," he said.

Hugging goodbye in the parking lot, he took my hand and placed it on him. "See what you do to me."

"Your actions never match your words," I said as he kissed me more, with the same passion and fury as before.

• • •

Birds sang the bright, sunny, summer afternoon away as I drove the white work minivan north on Route 66. Relentlessly I cried, wishing Alexander were alive. The only person I wanted to talk to. The only one who'd understand.

• • •

On one side of the paper I drew charcoal-colored trees and mountains. On the blank side, I scribbled "Happy Birthday." Carefully I placed it in between pages of a book, which was then stuffed in my bag before getting in "Grandpa," an old, gray Subaru. Grandpa's owner Maggie drove Ben and me up the winding mountain road. In the back seat I felt warm and lost in the blue sky.

Arriving, we walked past tiny, tan teepees built for kids to play in. Trees and streams with little wooden bridges ran alongside them. Dillon sat at a picnic table near the stage, camera in hand, filming the band. I took my place on the same side as him. Our legs gently rested against each other as the songs filled the air and sunk deeper inside me than music had done before. Wanting to dance, I spun alone at first, then was joined by an elderly man with silver hair and overalls who stepped sweetly and lightly alongside me.

I felt Dillon's gaze the entire time and went to him after a few songs. "Let's go inside," he whispered. I agreed, wanting moments of solitude with him too.

When the sun started to drop and the end of August night cooled, Maggie, Ben, and I joined Dillon for a joint in his bus. Ben stood outside the open doors, while Maggie sat with Dillon and me on the seat inside the bus. At some point, I discreetly slipped Dillon his card and he found my hand, secretly holding it behind our backs. This felt different than being kissed by him. Different than anything with anyone, ever.

Down the dark swirling mountain road, I longed for him,

wishing I could have stayed. That I could curl into him for warmth while we slept in his bus. That we could wake up in the fresh dewy air and prepare for a fun-filled day, just the two of us.

Back at home and alone in my dimly lit dining room, unable to sleep from lust and alcohol, I poured one more drink and let the art empty out of me. A sketch of hands entwined.

My muse, I thought.

Before bed I wrote to him, "Goodnight!"

"Come back up and hike with me tomorrow!" he said.

"It's your 40th, don't you want to be with your friends!?"

"I want to be with you."

"Okay!"

Dillon drove us to the entrance of North South Lake. "Wait here, I'll go see what's up with parking," he said. Watching him walk to the little booth, Lando on my lap, I felt the most myself, which momentarily masked my grief and replaced it with one thought.

This could be my life.

Steps into the hike, before it was humanly possible for the tiny amount of mushrooms to kick in, a wave of panic rushed over me. *What am I doing? I shouldn't be here. I love Zak.* The thought was instantly swept away though, stacked in a place reserved for things I couldn't comprehend.

On the peak of the mountain, Dillon and I ate Welch's Fruit Snacks and spoke about love. His wedding and divorce. His daughters. Then about death, which had molded me but had not yet touched him. As we stood to start our descent, some combination of us and our openness in nature made the full weight of what I had become over the years very clear.

Numb.

The truth was ripped from inside of me out into the universe.

"I feel like I just woke up. Like, what was I doing?"

Back at the lot, Dillon said, "Follow me for a few drinks? I know the perfect place."

Driving down the foothill, he veered right where I had always gone left. When he turned into an almost empty lot, I parked near him, facing a small red shed. Behind us stood a red-brick bar with a tin roof. A post near the road held a small, circular sign. Inside the circle was an oil painting; a couple engulfed in muted-green trees, looking out over a ledge toward blue hills.

Above them, the name of the bar was painted.

"Kindred Spirits."

We pulled our Adirondack chairs closer to the unlit fire pit; our feet rested on top of the cinder blocks, touching. Our conversations, even after a day of hiking, were stimulating while still calm and comfortable. As I listened intently to him, my left hand gently held his bicep. His strength of both body and mind gave me the intimacy my soul so desperately desired.

At dusk, between our vehicles, we kissed goodbye.

"I wish the timing of us were better," he said.

"I don't know...you always say, 'Trust the universe.' Maybe we met exactly when we were supposed to."

"True! We should probably still slow down with the sexual stuff though," he said, kissing me more.

"We should wait," he said again, then kissed my neck, sliding his hand up my thigh, behind my shorts.

"See, I told you, your words never match your actions!"

"I can't help it. This is what you do to me," he said, taking my hand and placing it on him again.

"Should we wait?" I asked.

"Shouldn't we?"

"We could die on the way home," I said.

He led me into the bus.

Lying naked after, he shyly pulled a white sheet over his body so that only his chest and arms were slightly exposed.

"You don't have to do that. Not in front of me," I said.

・ ・ ・

To my journal I confessed, *"I was too broken to be in my marriage. Too broken when we got together. I never healed from my past.*

Is that all an excuse?

Even if I changed now, I can never be honest with Zak. It will hurt him too much.

I have to leave.

Then heal and be a better person going forward.

Give Zak the opportunity to leave and be better too, without destroying him with my truth. I love him. I believe in him. We are just so different. I knew that all along but...love.

Love can't fix what I've already fucked up too much.

Is that my final decision? GO FOR A WALK AND FIGURE IT OUT."

Walking couldn't help. I was so sad at who I was.

I wrote more. *"Is this all because of drinking? Did I trick myself into falling for Dillon to justify a drunken mistake? Dear Universe, please give me clarity to find the voice inside of me to follow. To be kind and good to everyone. Including myself. I try but I fail and hurt the ones I love. Fuck. BE MINDFUL. One decision away. Knowledge to action. ACTION. What story do I want to tell? Is it wrong to think of any of it as a story? Was Dillon put here to make Zak and I grow into the people we were meant to be, together? Or is Dillon a soul mate? He feels like one. What is the purpose of Dillon and I...Are these my true words? I always wonder that. Why don't I ever know my own truth? What is true?*

Truth: If I fuck up one more time, I will kill myself.

Actually, I don't know if that's true. The only thing I know

for certain is:
   I NEED TO BE HONEST.
   TRUTH OR DIE."

· · ·

For twenty-two days after that, Dillon and I spoke daily. Most mornings I sent him some sort of art that was symbolic to us—a sketch of an anime man and woman in bed, her head on his chest, her hand through it, holding his heart. The dialogue bubble above them read, "Real or Not Real."

"Real," Dillon wrote back.

During the day we'd sneak to parks to say hello. At night we crept to adjacent towns for privacy, no longer pretending with each other we were only friends.

"Come to my sister's! They have a music festival on their farm every year!"

His family was easy and natural too and again, I thought:
This could be my life.

· · ·

On the twenty-third day a new therapist answered me back with a few questions. Instantly, I replied, *"As far as my issues...maybe existential anxiety? I think that has been an issue since I was little. I was suicidal/depressed from about 15-23, and never had any formal type of help (like therapy or medication). I had some pretty traumatic relationships that I should have healed from and maybe didn't—then got married and now am struggling with what I did in the last 8 years, mainly drinking which led to cheating. Now I feel like I have to leave my marriage, for his sake (and mine). So, I am struggling with that. In a nutshell, marriage, drinking and behavioral issues...and making it so I don't feel like there is no point to anything because we all just* die anyway. I don't want to keep making the same mistakes in my life that I did since I was a teenager. That is insane. Sorry if that was too much."

He responded right back, "Ha! No, not at all—never too much information as far as I'm concerned! I appreciate your honesty and am sorry to hear you've been struggling. Trauma is disruptive to our sense of authentic self-connection in many ways, ways that we can talk about, and work on, moving forward."

He felt like an old friend I was having an intelligent conversation with. Eventually, the unavoidable word—trauma—came up. I explained that the first therapist asked me that too and when I said I didn't know if I had any she told me, "If you're unsure, you probably do," which I thought was kind of strange to say.

"But did it change your mind? Or did your definition of trauma change? You mentioned it in your email."

"I still wouldn't call anything I went through traumatic. I wasn't raped at gunpoint or anything," I laughed.

"It can look different."

"Yeah…I guess…But I never felt like it was my own. Like I didn't have a right to it."

"Does something feel like it belongs to you now?"

"I guess what I meant in my email was that I should've healed after I dated a crackhead who put me twenty grand in debt!" I laughed and then briefly explained Nate. Our addictions. Suicide pacts. I accidentally trailed off toward things I hadn't thought about since they happened. "It wasn't always paint thinner for breakfast. Before Florida, before that, Nate made us pancakes. But even then, it wasn't normal. I should have known to leave."

"How do you mean, *not normal*?" he asked.

"Like, his ex-girlfriend, the mother to his child, chased me around his dining room table with a knife."

"How did you feel after?"

"I don't remember."

"You don't remember, it sounds scary."

"She was a drug addict. I felt sad for her. Honestly, I never spoke about it after it happened because I guess it felt like nothing compared to everything else."

"How do you feel right now?"

"I guess I hate that question. I don't know how to answer it, ever. Every emotion and nothing too. Like I am waiting for the soul-crushing cries to come. I know I deserve them. I almost miss them in a weird way. At least then I knew what I felt."

"Well, what about if I ask how you feel about Nate?"

"I don't regret Nate. It needed to happen for me to know I wouldn't kill myself. The opportunity was there. My depression, the worse it could be. And I didn't do it."

"What did you do after Florida?"

"I just moved back to New York."

"You didn't talk to anyone about it?"

"Not really. Oh wait, actually I did see a therapist once when I came back! He asked me to role play. Like he pretended to be Nate and asked what I would say to him. I wasn't into it and never went back."

"Was there a reason you chose New York?"

"Yeah. My parents and sister live here."

"You didn't talk with them?"

"Not really. My mom doesn't know how to have a serious conversation. I can be like, 'My best friend died,' and she'd literally say, 'Oh look at this new plant.'"

"Do you have a good relationship with her?"

"Yes, I love her!"

"How do you feel when she switches topics on you?"

"I'm never mad at her. She's amazing in her own ways."

"Did your mother have her own trauma?"

"Oh my god yes. Her sister died of AIDS, which I've heard was from being raped but then other people said heroin. I never asked. We didn't talk about it. My mom did heroin too. She apologized to me a few years ago for doing it while she was pregnant with me. She said she did it the day I was born, in the bathroom of her hospital room. My dad said that wasn't true, but he wasn't there. My aunt Karen went with my mom, not him."

"How did you feel when your mother told you that?"

"I laughed when she told me not to tell my sister. She thought Jamie'd be mad at her. I think she knew I wouldn't. A few days later, I felt relieved. Like I found a little piece of the puzzle."

"The puzzle?"

"Of what was wrong with me. Like maybe I had actual brain chemistry stuff wrong with me from her using drugs. I googled long term effects on babies addicted to heroin, trying to find a study or something linking it to depression, but never did."

"Find what was wrong with you?"

"I guess that stuck from when I was a teenager. I kept journals to figure out what was wrong with me, why I was sad when I shouldn't have been. Sometimes I thought it was from doing too much ecstasy, like it ate a hole in my brain, but I was sad before that."

"Did your mom talk any more about when you were born?"

"Not really. Well except once more actually. Like a year later at TJ Maxx she told some woman who had a tiny newborn how I was so tiny when I was born too. Four pounds. Then she told the lady I had to stay in the hospital for a while after because of it."

"Did you know that?"

"I knew I was little, but not that I stayed in the hospital."

"What did you say then?"

"I laughed and was like, 'Wow, Mom, did you come visit me at all?'"

"Did she?"

"She said she did!"

"How did that feel, to find that out?"

"It just felt like another piece of the puzzle too. It made me think of the experiment with the Harlow monkeys, ya know, how the baby monkeys felt better with cloth on the fake metal mom monkeys. Like was I just alone in a cold crib when I was first born? Was that why I had weird attachment issues, or non-attachment maybe?"

"And that doesn't make you upset with your mom?"

"No. Not at all. She did her best and she's good at showing love in different ways."

"Do you wish you could talk more about that with your parents?"

"No. It really doesn't matter anyway and we've never been a family who talks like that."

"You know, it's possible because of your mother's own trauma she can't process when you share yours. She may switch to plants because she can't talk about harder things. What you are saying could literally be too much for her to hear, so she doesn't. Imagine your words floating over her head," he said, motioning with his hand, my pain moving over his own.

"I never thought of it that way."

My entire life I thought I held everything inside because of something that was solely wrong with me. That I had a defect that made me unable to connect or share in an authentic way. A way that could have allowed my parents or someone to help me when I wanted to die. For the first time, I was seeing the picture as a whole, as ways my family helped shape my ability to communicate. Maybe none of us knew how to do it or had the tools to talk about stuff in the way we needed. Maybe that's why I only knew how to write what I felt. With no resentment toward my parents, this new insight did allow me the smallest amount of understanding and maybe even forgiveness toward myself.

Maybe my lack of communication skills was what was wrong with me.

· · ·

Less than a week after that appointment, I sat still on the seat of my bike, kickstand down, feet on the pedals. My hands on the handlebars, tears streaming down my face.

"Love, what's wrong?" Zak said as he walked out back, catching me by surprise.

"Nothing," I said.

"Tell me."

Quiet for a few moments, he waited for me to speak. When I didn't, he sat at the round teak table next to me and asked more sternly, "Amy, just tell me what's wrong."

"I don't know how."

"Just say it," he said.

Not able to look at him, I leaned forward on the front bar of my bike and rested my head on my forearms. Tears poured onto the light-gray patio below me, turning it dark.

So many more times, he said, "Just say it."

And so I did.

"I cheated."

"What the fuck. With who?" he asked.

"Amy, with who?" he asked, again.

"Jordan."

"What the fuck. When?"

"Two years ago," I answered.

"When we were fucking married. We were already married, Amy."

Although unsure why I started there, I could see it was enough. He left.

An outcome I understood and expected.

Maybe I wouldn't need to tell him about Dillon.

Why hurt him more when he was already gone?

Alone, I journaled, *"The truth sets you free. Yes. First it kills. Tiny deaths. In trying so hard to avoid hurting people, I did it more so. I want to be free of that person. The person I was my whole life. I want to learn from it all and move on. I will be someone Zak used to know, and that is heartbreaking. Life is. Does nothing matter?*

If everything matters, I will be and deserve to be punished for this. I will be fucked for my actions. I do not deserve a new start when I've hurt other people.

Still my dreaded default setting soothes me—the comforting notion that maybe one day I will kill myself. When I'm old. After my parents are gone. When my body starts to give and there really is no one left to disappoint. Nothing left to do. Still my sister might be here...I won't do that to her.

If nothing matters though, maybe the universe won't punish me. Maybe that only works if I don't punish myself with self-defeating thoughts and actions. Todd said, 'You don't have to be punished or suffer, you are making amends by moving on. You deserve to be free.' I PRAY that is true. And I hate the word 'deserve.' No one deserves anything. Zak doesn't deserve this. He will be okay though. He is better than me on every level."

The House

With each breakup, for months or even years before it actually happened, I'd envision the other person better after us. Sober. Happy. Successful. Whatever flaw they had, they fixed, while I stayed the same, some sort of broken. It was no different with Zak.

My whole heart felt he'd find a young, beautiful bride. She'd give him a baby when they were both ready. They'd visit him behind the line in a kitchen he owned; he'd serve them something special, not offered on the menu. Opposite schedules wouldn't be a thing, she'd be a stay-at-home mom; they'd go to parks and other places together, on Tuesdays. Zak's day off. It would work out for him, I thought.

Not once in all of the scenarios did I imagine what was actually happening.

Zak dissected what he could have done differently, trying to find his fault so I'd forgive him.

"I should've gone to bed with you and not played video games," he said.

"It wasn't what you did, it was that I didn't know how to tell you I wasn't happy. It was me."

"Yeah, but you weren't happy because of me. Because of what I was doing."

To let him find peace with himself and hate me instead, I told him about Dillon. I owed him that.

To help him move on toward the life I created in my head for him.

• • •

Needing to get away from myself and the house, I asked Lando, "Wanna go for a ride?!" His ears perked and his tail wagged.

Driving toward Rev, we passed Elle, who was driving too, "Hi! We miss you!" she messaged me.

"I miss you! Lando and I are going for coffee and dog cookies!"

"Come here instead! I just made a pot."

Hanging out in the morning, with no alcohol, made me nervous but I said yes.

Elle cleaned up pans and dishes from breakfast while we chatted nonstop in non-sequiturs. Done inside, we sat on a step that led to her front door, absorbing the sun.

"Sorry I didn't tell you sooner it was Dillon," I confessed to Elle, who knew something had been going on, but not with whom.

"Oh my god, please don't feel bad about Dillon, we had no connection!" She laughed, then asked if I told Zak it was Dillon too.

"I did."

"How'd that go?"

"Ya know...as expected."

"Ugh. Life. I'm sorry. You can come here whenever you need if you get lonely. We're always home!"

"It's weird, the house actually feels less lonely now than when Zak was there. Like at least it makes sense to feel alone now."

"No, I get it. Besides being at work, he didn't hang out with you anyway. Like at Helsinki when he wouldn't even come with us for one. I hadn't seen him in forever either, so it felt weird. Like he didn't care."

"No way, he loves you, he cares. That's just him."

"You guys just seem on different levels."

"Yeah..."

"But it felt like you were always trying to make it work too. You were trying."

"I was...It doesn't matter though."

"It does."

"Everyone's going to hate me for what I did anyway."

Mostly, I hoped Elle didn't. She had been on the other side of this situation with Alexander, and I worried if somewhere in her mind, she thought I was terrible.

Driving home, I thought about how much I loved and needed that time with Elle. This in turn brought me back to what had haunted me since Alexander killed himself—how he always told me, "Go have dinner with Elle and the babies." And I didn't. Because my anxiety about being social without alcohol blinded me. It tricked me into always choosing to meet my regular crew for drinks instead of his family. That comfort, I now realized, was the reason I craved more meaningful relationships.

My thoughts drifted to the years that Zak's mother and sister invited me to bake Christmas cookies with them. Knowing they didn't drink, I declined there too, for fear I'd feel weird around them, in such a wholesome situation. Not knowing how to be with anyone but boyfriends without alcohol, made me wonder how many other meaningful connections I missed out on. It also made me reflect on the times I embarrassed myself with too much of my mask—words repeated, the end of nights unknown and mornings spent sending lighthearted apology texts to friends, "Sorry if I was annoying."

That was the person I thought was better than sober me?

For two decades, not only did I never challenge the seventh-grade notion that I liked me better with alcohol, I didn't think about it all. It was simply accepted and submerged into my being, propelled forward by ease and habit.

For the first time I could see, it wasn't true.

Sober me was better.

. . .

After separating from his wife, Eli moved back from Paris and worked with Zak and Isaac at Club Helsinki. The three of them mostly slept at Isaac's, minus the times I came home to find Eli on my couch, at my dining room table, or in the backyard, smoking.

"Why did you drop him off here?" I asked Zak.

"He asked me to," Zak answered, annoyed.

"Are you upset?"

"Not upset, but it doesn't feel good leaving MY best friend at MY house, with MY wife."

Over the years Eli spent countless nights with us, sometimes for weeks at a time. He and I became close too, bonding over both being good at the bar, sharing the knack for befriending any person because of a genuine curiosity about their life. Eli was one of my favorite people to talk to, yet it still felt unwarranted for him to be at the house, nonchalantly telling me things without me asking:

Zak's Tinder profile.

The hot, younger-than-me therapist Zak had sex with.

"I had drinks with them. She's in love with him already!"

"Of course she is! Why wouldn't she be," I said.

KNOWING I HAD no right to be upset with any of it, I still casually brought it up to Zak on our walk.

"I heard you have a sexy new therapist."

"What did you expect me to do, Amy?"

"I don't know. That. I guess."

"I didn't want to. All I fucking wanted was you."

"Why are you doing it then?"

"That's what everyone said I should do. Hook up with girls to get over you."

"I get it. It just seems like if you don't want to do that, you shouldn't. But do what makes you happy."

"I was happy. With you."

"You were happy the whole time?"

"Yes. I love you."

"That confuses me more. Like, how did we feel so different in the same relationship?"

"I don't know. It doesn't have to matter. I want to go on hikes and adventures with you now."

"You say that, but I don't want to force you. If you're only doing it for me, eventually you'll go back to normal. You can't fake it forever."

"I do want to do those things."

"I just feel like I'm a yes person and you're a no person. I say let's do something and you create a million reasons why we can't. Even dog walks, you'll say you don't have the right shoes or whatever. I think you just don't like those things, and that's okay. We're just different."

"I do like those things. I'm trying to be better. To stop myself from being lazy. I know you like Dillon because of the bus and wanting adventures and to travel. I want to do those things with you."

Topics Zak got overly upset about in the past came up too. Instead of getting defensive or angry though, he listened when I again apologized for my relationship with money. "It was hard being the responsible one. I didn't mind paying for vacations or whatever, but it was a lot of pressure to be the one who had to keep the serious job so we'd have health insurance and savings while you got to do whatever you wanted."

"I'm sorry, I get it. I do."

"I'm sorry too. I didn't mean to be like that. It's just that I worked so hard getting out of debt from Nate and other people, it made me weird about money, but more than that I needed you to be able to talk to me about serious stuff without getting mad, like you are now."

On the dusty stone-path portion of the trail, almost back to the parking lot, I realized how different it felt with Zak after having a real conversation. I thanked him for it. "Stay for a beer?" I asked when we were back in the yard too.

"Sure!"

We sat in the green plastic Adirondack chairs, untying our hiking boots. The almost-autumn grass felt fluffy and good on my feet. The wind was warm, gently blowing the wind chimes that hung in our tree, where Zak had proposed five years prior.

"Did Dillon ever spend the night here?"

"Why would you ask that," I said.

"Just tell me. Did he?"

"We drank too much a couple of times...His house was too far to drive back to."

"He slept in our fucking bed. The one thing I asked you not to do." He stood. Stormed off as I said, "Wait." The dust from the driveway had barely settled before he wrote, "You destroyed me. I wish I was man enough to hug you before I left. I'll miss that."

Then there were the suicide texts.

Eli was with me, sitting at the dining room table, assuring me Zak wouldn't do anything.

"You look worse than he does," Eli said.

"Maybe he needs to date a better therapist," I joked.

"See! You're fine, he's going to be fine, now can we please leave this house for food. I'm dying, yo."

"I don't want to go anywhere. Or see people. What if he's not fine?"

"Zak isn't going to do anything. I'm hungover as fuck. Please, Moth."

Moth was the nickname given to me by Eli. I loved it for some reason and agreed to go with him, despite having no appetite. My only pretext was we had to go where we'd likely not know anyone. I couldn't pretend to be okay.

Hours went by where Eli and I sat at a bar and Zak wouldn't

respond. When he finally did, he said, "Where are you guys? I'm at the house."

"Eli wanted food. We'll leave in a minute."

"Glad you're out having fun."

"You weren't answering us. I didn't know what to do."

"Whatever, Amy."

"Where were you?" I asked.

"Sitting in my fucking car on the fucking train tracks, but glad you're happy."

Zak showed me burns on his chest from holding a lighter to his body. He crumbled to the kitchen floor, theatrically crying. For once, I did not feel sympathy or sad; I was mad he threatened suicide after Alexander, after knowing my past too. His performance felt baited, as if to say, "Look what you did to me, now suffer too." Which was fine, I would. I was. Just don't use those words, that threat.

He claimed to be too drunk to drive home and too hurt to sleep in the house, so he slept in the car, parked in the driveway. In the morning, not wanting to face Eli on the couch, I stayed captive in bed. I wondered what was wrong with me. Why I would think Zak was acting. I had done it before too. During sex, I looked up at him wondering if those were really the sounds and faces he wanted to make or was it a show. Was he doing what he thought he should be doing instead of what he felt? For the first time, I thought my disbelief might be a reflection of my own disconnection. Was I detached and projecting?

. . .

The next time Zak came over he carried clear plastic bins into his gaming room; he stood in front of his dresser and closet, filling them. In bed, I watched from across the hall. When he came in to say goodbye, I told him, "I tried," hoping he would understand, despite what I had done, that I loved him and wished it had happened differently, wished I were better.

"Tried how, Amy?"

"To move. To find a job where we could have more time together. I just needed something to change," I said, trailing off into the thought that I would have had a baby with him too.

With Zak gone, I stayed in bed, knees to my chest, tears soaking Bunny resting below my head in place of a pillow, paralyzed by what I had done and who I had become. Liking Dillon didn't take away how terrible losing my husband was.

Waking up, feeling the fog that comes after the deep sleep tied to depression, I reached for my phone to find the time and saw a message from Dillon: "Good morning. Meet me and the girls at the brewery later?"

"Hi. I thought you didn't let people meet the girls. You don't have to offer that."

"I want you to," Dillon wrote back.

"What if they don't like me haha!" I wrote, anxious that they'd sense my sadness, that I might not be happy or fun enough to be around kids. Around anyone.

"Of course they'll like you, they're mini me's!"

Same as with their dad and his sister's farm, it was easy and natural. *This could be my life*, I thought. Again.

• • •

Driving back from Dillon and the girls, I took my shoes and socks off and blasted the heat onto the bare skin of my feet as I thought about how strange the universe was—to go from crying in bed over a baby I didn't have, to that. To what felt like possibility, like hope for love and family.

Almost home, my phone vibrated. Expecting it to be Dillon, I was surprised to see it was Nate. "Hi! My mom bought a house on your parents' road in Stottville. I'm here now! Say hello?"

It had been years since I heard from him and at least ten

since we had seen each other, but because of the day, I said sure anyway. Nate knocked on the window before I turned the car off. "How did you know it was me in here?"

"I saw you pull in!"

"I can't find my socks!"

"You need socks, I'll give you my socks right now! I'll take them off my feet and give them to you!" He said in the same manic but endearing tone.

Inside, I ordered drinks while he sipped something nonalcoholic. He showed me his phone, a picture of him and his fiancé. They were on her parents' yacht. Stunning in her swimsuit, I jokingly asked Nate how he hit the lottery with someone like her. He explained they met at AA but her alcohol addiction wasn't really that bad. It didn't ruin lives, like his did.

"I'm so sorry for what I did," he said.

"You don't have to be. I was never mad at you."

"I know you weren't. That's what makes it so bad. You know, I speak in front of huge crowds of people in recovery, all over Boston, talking about you. About us. Hoping to help."

"Really? You talk about Florida?"

"Of course."

"I don't know why, but it makes me feel better to hear you say that. Like, obviously it was crazy but hearing you say it means more. Like it was real."

"It was real."

"I know, I guess."

"I still haven't known anyone like you," Nate said.

"I'm really not that special," I laughed.

"You are. Do you know anyone like you?"

"Um. I don't know," I laughed again.

"What's going on with your fiancé, aren't you happy?"

"I'd leave her right now for you!"

"No! Don't say that. What's going on?"

"Our only rule is not to lie and she did."

"Talk to her about it!"

"I know...it's just crazy. We have an open relationship because she's into, like, hitting and stuff. She wants me to, like, punch her in the face and strangle her. I can't do it. Sometimes I'll just be in the other room doing fantasy baseball while she's with some dude. I really don't care."

"Oh my god," I laughed.

"What happened with Jackie?" I asked.

"Oh my god! It got crazy! Bad. We got into heroin. I was on the news for armed robbery! I went to prison!"

"What the fuck!"

"I know! It was insane! I shouldn't have done that to you. Any of it."

"It's okay!"

"Thank you for saying that, pretty head."

We hugged goodbye but before I made it home, Nate sent me one more message. "Should I come over? It's the only time I'll ask."

"I can't. I'm sorry," I said.

I didn't hear from Nate again but found comfort in hoping our story of suffering in Florida wasn't for nothing—if it helped people in recovery heal, our love mattered.

We mattered.

I just hoped Nate found the closure he needed. To be free of me. Of it all. To be married and happy.

. . .

I'm not sure exactly why Zak and I were at my dad's shop. Maybe unloading something into the dumpster or borrowing a truck. We were in separate vehicles though. While we walked back toward them Zak said, "What you're saying is you love me but you're not in love with me?"

"I guess so," I said.

Looking in Zak's room, the floor was filled with clothes. Collections of belts, hats, and swords hung on the walls. The windowsills were still lined with empty *Game of Thrones* beer bottles. Figurines like The Crow and Rick and Morty were on top of his tall dresser. I wanted it all gone. Not only because I hated the mess, but because the in between was killing me. The constant guilt and reminders of what I did were too much.

Standing in the living room, I took the only picture of us off the wall—my back bronzed and bare besides Zak's hands, which were wrapped around me while I stood tiptoe on volcanic lava fragments, kissing him as the pink sunset kissed the ocean. Crying, I tucked it away in the guest room and packed the rest of us into the third dresser drawer—ten years of homemade cards and one photo album from our first year together.

Add Water, Will Grow

"I think I had a headache for three or four weeks and I don't know if I got my period last month. Time feels like a blur."

"A blur?" the therapist asked.

"Yeah, like, I know I went to brunch Saturday then for cider Sunday, but, in general, time and days feel weird and blended. Quick and slow. I don't know."

"How's your drinking been?"

"I had a few beers before I came here. I've done that before every one of our appointments. Is that bad?"

"No. It doesn't have to mean that."

Instead of a questionnaire, we talked about drinking smarter.

"What if you add water in between drinks?" he asked.

"I've planned to do that before, like in my head, before I go places. But once I start drinking, I forget. I wish I'd remember after drink three or four!"

"Why then?"

"I want at least a tiny buzz!"

"Are you drinking to have fun?"

"Yeah, I guess so. It's like the only way I know how to socialize. When I want people, I go for drinks."

"More than three or four drinks?"

"Yeah. That's the problem. Sometimes, I stay too long and drink too much, till it's not fun. Not always. But when I do, I do."

"Your brain will tell you to drink. You might think it's because you are wanting to go out and have fun, have a good time, but subconsciously drinking is how you deal with stress, so your brain is tricking you into going because you are so stressed."

The next night, when Dillon offered to pick me up, I knew that desire drove me to Dillon, not stress. When we arrived at the bar though, I ordered a water with my vodka while explaining my plan—a glass between each drink. Dillon offered his solidarity, but our water glasses sat, sweating, weathering the paper coaster into a soggy mess, untouched except for the first few sips. In the morning, I was relieved to wake up with only a strong thirst, not a real hangover.

Maybe I'll tattoo a watering can on my hand so I see it when I take a sip, I thought.

Maybe with a little flower too.

A constant reminder:

ADD WATER. WILL GROW.

. . .

"I'm debating if I should eat dinner or have Skippits," Dillon wrote.

"Wait, Skippits?! Like skip it?"

"Haha yep! That's what my dad always gave us when my mom wasn't home!"

It was such a dad line. Alexander and I always sent each other dad lines.

"Aww. Poor little kid, you!" I said.

"Haha…I know right?! Also, is it Wednesday yet?"

Wednesday was a line left over from when we sometimes only had that day together. When it changed and we saw each other all week, it mostly meant we wished we could be together. An "I miss you," but better.

"No, but tomorrow is October. Should we celebrate!?" I asked.

"I think so! It seems right!"

"Tacos?" I asked.

"Our place or Magdalena's?"

"I'm down for anything! I love our little place, but it's far for you. Magdalena's is close and we've never been! I'm bad at picking!"

"I'll do it for you then! I'll come get you after work. We'll go to our spot."

My left leg between his legs, we sipped tequila and talked about the difference between men being masculine in a respectful way and being a dick. I thanked him for being the former, for making me feel taken care of in a nice way.

Driving me home, he turned down Mt. Merino road.

"Why are we going this way?" I asked.

"I want to show you something, a surprise!"

In the dark drizzle, Dillon entered a code. The gate slowly opened, his headlights illuminating the modern mansion. "It's the house I just finished!"

Holding my hand, he led me inside and handed me a beer from the stocked refrigerator. Leafing through the brochure on the counter, where the price tag for the river view home was close to a million, I said, "This is insane! You're so talented!"

"Come, I'll show you around!"

In a secret side room, my socks somehow became completely covered in sawdust, making us laugh so hard. Taking them off to keep the house clean, I followed Dillon up the stairs, built by him. In the master suite, we made love to the sound of rain dancing on the tin roof above us.

...

A few days later, in an empty and dark parking lot across the street from Wunderbar, Dillon and I sat in his white truck as he asked, "Something on your mind, babe?"

Starting to speak, I stopped myself.

"What is it?"
"Nothing, it's dumb!"
"Say it."
"No, it's stupid."
"Tell me. You can say anything to me."
"Everyone keeps saying you'll leave me the second Pip wants you back."

He took my face into his hands and kissed me. Still so close to my lips, he softly said, "I would never do that to you. You have such a kind, sweet soul. I would never do it. You treat me the way I always wanted Pip to. You make me feel the way I should. I'm not going anywhere."

• • •

After that, whole weekends were spent together. Friday the farm for beers. Saturday his hand on my leg in a dark auditorium before he went on stage with Ben and Phil. I watched them in an audience full of people I'd known and loved my whole life, thinking how perfectly our worlds fit. Sunday, we ate Adderall and I made him promise me he wasn't a drug addict. At the brewery, we sat outside at a picnic table, literally speaking nonstop.

Monday, I sent him a text from my desk. "I feel like my heart is going to explode! We need a break from drinks!"

"Come over, I'll hug you so you feel better and cook you dinner."

We snuggled on his loveseat watching *Straight Outta Compton*. I felt full from it all.

• • •

Dillon invited me to parks to play with the girls and farms for apple cider donuts. Eating pizza, a couple across from us said, "You guys are such a cute family."

The night of Hopper's annual Halloween party, Dillon asked

if I wanted to carve pumpkins with the girls. My heart was happy to have something more. I sent Hopper a message. "Hi! I might not come tonight, not really feeling a party. Dillon's bringing the girls over. Plus, I don't have a costume for once!"

"I totally get it. If you change your mind, come without one or we totally have stuff you can wear too!"

MAKING SURE THE house was the best it could be for their first visit, I stocked cider, beer, and wine so Dillon had options; animal crackers, goldfish, fruit, and veggies so the girls did too. We looked for Waldo in my books before carving Paw Patrol pumpkins. When Dillon went to pick up dinner, the girls stayed with me, coloring in a Precious Moments book, leftover from when I was their age. After we ate, Dillon and I were instructed to sit together for a dance performance to Dropkick Murphy type tunes. We watched Halloween cartoons before it was time to go. In the empty house, wishing they could have stayed the night, I messaged Hopper. "Hey, still hanging?!"

"Yes! Just so you know Heather was trying to make a big deal you didn't come earlier. She saw Dillon's truck at your house."

"Haha. Well, they left."

. . .

Curled up with a light blanket, I answered FaceTime. "See, I knew you'd answer for me!" Dillon teased, knowing I hated pictures, videos, and therefore FaceTime. We spoke about going on some sort of weekend away, to the sea or grove.

Later in the week we said good night earlier than we traditionally did, concluding the conversation with me telling him, "I'll send you the links for the cabins I found! There's a cute one in Woodstock."

In the morning, I drove a minivan full of coworkers to the

same training space I had been to years before—where I panicked about Alexander, about wasting time and life. Sitting there, I hated it just as much the second time around. It felt fake and forced again. The same type of introductions and icebreakers. Similar strategies to working with families.

On a fifteen-minute break before lunch, I looked at my phone and found a message from Charlotte. "Hi."

"Hi!" I wrote back.

"A very reliable source said Dillon's truck was at Pip's house this morning."

Wondering why she would tell on her best friend, she answered without me saying it. "I'm so sick of them and this. It's so ridiculous. I don't want you to be hurt and lied to."

Pacing the parking lot, I knew what Charlotte meant. My gut said it was true too. She and Pip were best friends, there was no reason it wouldn't be.

"Hello," I messaged Dillon.

He didn't respond, something he had never done since we met.

Holding back tears and feeling flushed, I went back into the training late. Silently I sat there, surrounded by my peers, thinking, *I hate this fucking building. Something bad always happens in it.* Unable to concentrate, my ears felt hot. My heart actually ached.

"I'M AT TRAINING on Marcus Boulevard. Come get me?" I asked Whitney, who left DSS for a state job, in Albany.

"Did something happen?"

"Dillon...Pip..."

"Of course I'll come get you."

Giving the keys to a coworker named Carly, I said someone else would have to drive them home.

Whitney stopped at the nearest gas station for drinks and cigs to get me through the forty-minute ride home. Driving again, she said, "I can't believe he's not answering you."

"I guess everyone was right," I said.

"He's so fucking stupid, Pip is going to do the same thing she always does to him. She just didn't like that he was happy with you. She knows what she's doing."

"I'm so stupid. I honestly wasn't worried about her."

In my driveway, Whitney asked if she should stay.

"Nah, I'm okay."

By the time I saw the message from Ben, it was dark out and my buzz was keeping me from crying, "Hey. We were just with Dillon. He told us what happened. Hope you're ok."

"That's nice he told you before speaking to me," I responded.

"What the fuck. He came over to Kaia and Phil's and we specifically asked if he already talked to you. He said he did."

"Well, obviously he is more worried about the band and making sure you guys are good than me."

"I'm sorry. We wouldn't have let him explain if we knew he didn't talk to you yet. You ok?"

"No worries. Yeah, I'm fine," I said to Ben and then messaged Dillon, "That's cool you are telling my friends before you even respond to me."

He wrote back, vague and unapologetic.

The following night, on actual Halloween, the plan was for Whitney, Heather, Maggie and me to hand out candy at Sean's house in Wartman's Square, Halloween haven. Instead though, I stayed home and spoke to Dillon on the phone. For over an hour, he never said sorry or admitted he was choosing Pip. "I have to focus on myself and the girls. My attention needs to be getting better for them, on being a good dad."

There was no point in me saying, "I forgive you. We can move on," because he wasn't asking for it. I had already become figurative to him.

He said, "You showed me how I deserved to be treated. You raised the bar for any girl after you."

"Anyone after you" was a weird thing to say. I knew he was choosing Pip, which I couldn't be mad at.

At love.

He loved her.

I loved him.

Zak loved me.

It was a cruel little cycle.

"This would be easier if you were yelling at me," he said before we started to say goodbye.

"I'm not mad. Just sad," I said.

Inside, music still played from the living room speaker, but I didn't hear a single song or think a thought. I sat at the dining room table, head down on my arms, folded into myself, crying. Letting years of pain pour out.

. . .

As hot water washed over me, I cried at the sight of my breasts because they reminded me of Dillon, the first boy to pick that as his favorite part of me. To stop the tears I switched my focus. "I'm so lucky to have running water. To shower. To have work to go to."

When I forced myself to finally eat, tears ran into my scrambled eggs. I embraced it and replaced it, "Thank you to the farmers that cared for the chickens. Thank you to the chickens who gave me the eggs."

On the kettle, I pressed the black lever. The tiny circular cover of the spout lifted, steam swirled out, misting my face. Inhaling it into my lungs, I thought, *I'm thankful to breathe.*

Pouring the hot water over ground coffee beans, I told myself, "I am lucky to afford this, to smell and taste it."

While walking Lando in the woods, I was thankful for my health. I thought of clients I worked with who didn't have that and told myself, "Be grateful. Others have it worse."

• • •

In the weeks after Halloween, people showed me pictures Pip and Dillon posted with the intention of wanting me to see how starved for attention and unauthentic they were.

"Ugh, look at this stupid picture," Whitney said, showing me something Dillon drew.

"I bought him that sketchbook," I said, feeling sad and deserving of it because I had a sketchbook bought for me by Zak, and in it were pictures I drew not only for Dillon, but *of* him. With pencils purchased while Zak stood next to me at Spotty Dog. Dillon and I were more similar than I wanted us to be.

Later, while sitting in my parents' living room, my sister showed me a post too. A picture with Dillon holding his youngest daughter's hand, the older one off in the foreground with Pip and her kids in a field full of Christmas trees. "I hate him," Jamie said.

I didn't. And I tried to replace the wanting with gratitude too, for my own family, but it wouldn't work. I only felt a loss for what I dreamt of—to be the one he drew pictures for again; to be the girl getting a tree with him and his daughters. To be the one who had my person to explore and enjoy the earth with.

All of it reminded me of how alone I felt before him and made me think that maybe I was destined to feel that way forever, a solitary soul unable to compete with what Pip offered—a big, blended house full of love, laughter, and life from her and her little ones too. *I understand why he chose her. I would have too*, I thought.

• • •

Clients became my daily crutch for gratitude, swallowing my time and humbling me further.

George was old and blind. He hated people but liked me. One home visit he asked, "Got any kids?"

"Nope, just a dog!"

"Oh, you're smart then!"

"Yeah, I hear that a lot actually. It still surprises me that people say that!"

"Did I ever tell you I had a daughter named Amy?"

"No!"

George explained he had three daughters.

All died in car accidents. At separate times.

"Amy was my fault though."

"I'm so sorry, George."

"I was supposed to get her but was too busy at work. I sent a driver. Amy was beautiful and the guy was trying to impress her, ya know, driving fast. My wife never forgave me for it."

When I wasn't with George, much of my time was spent with Jean. Jean's tub was stacked tall with boxes, old clothes draped over them. Her shower rod had no curtain, instead clothes hung from wire hangers. Despite this, Jean never smelled. Her kitchen counter and refrigerator held rotten food, expired and blue. The vinyl floor had droppings from mice. When she sat in her recliner, she was surrounded by stacks of papers and books. An old broken desk and lamps that didn't work were there too. She always apologized for the mess.

Jean didn't want to leave her home but eventually she agreed to go to doctor appointments with me. Then to take a tour of an assisted living program. Each time we left her trailer, she'd ask, "Do I look okay? I'm just going to brush my hair once more."

The day I brought her boxes and asked her to slowly collect some things, she cried. Trying to help her, we pushed the spare bedroom door open, barely fitting through, "Most of this stuff belongs to my daughters. My eldest owned the trailer. I moved in when she was diagnosed with cancer. Before she died."

Jean said some of the other stuff she held onto for her other daughter. "She might come home one day and want it."

Jean didn't know I knew her living daughter, Darlene; that a few times a year I visited Darlene because Social Services stood in as Darlene's Guardian, after Darlene suffered a traumatic brain injury. Jean couldn't remember that Darlene would never leave the facility she resided in, that she was never coming for the book bag and boxes Jean packed for her.

Then there was Alessandro. His anxiety had him neglect going for checkups after a failed suicide attempt and later, heart attack. My comfort in taking him to various appointments was selfish in that I found great relief in not having to speak when I was sad, since Alessandro was deaf and did all the talking.

While we met with doctors, I wrote everything down for Alessandro, who never learned to sign or read lips. Afterwards, Alessandro would cry and thank me for taking him places and for being kind. On a day that I thought to myself, *Anyone can do your job...You aren't doing anything special*, Alessandro said, "You're different from anyone else. Nicer. You never get mad at me for talking too loud or anything." He was helping me too.

They all were, which was why when the workday ended, they stayed in my thoughts as I walked to the river, forcing myself to acknowledge how lucky I was to be there. To have a body that worked. My health. To have a single family member or friend when people like Alessandro literally had none. They, and other clients too, constantly reminded me, I was fortunate to have the capacity to contemplate any of this too, to have my mind. To look out into the wilderness and think, *I am me...I was this before Dillon and will continue to be after.*

Back from the woods and before bed, with a clearer head, I laughed at Lando, rolling around like a goon. I thought how he was the furthest thing from Broadus, my old, serious soul, but his message and life lesson were clear—in a world full of loss and tragedy, I could love something as much, but differently.

. . .

The combination of my appointments only being scheduled every other week, my tendency to cancel and how fast everything changed made it so my therapist was in more shock than me when I told him what happened.

"You mentioned Dillon was the first time your gut screamed DO THIS. How does it feel that it was wrong?"

"I don't think it was wrong."

"Tell me about that?"

"Dillon needed to happen. My heart needed to be broken."

"Why did it need to be broken?"

"To show me I could be so sad and not want to kill myself. Knowing I wouldn't is different than knowing I wouldn't want to."

"And now you know?"

"Yes. I'm not afraid to feel sad now."

"It's hard to have someone you feel so connected to be gone unexpectedly. You do seem to have a good take on it though."

"Maybe I confuse soul mates for those who I suffer something with, hit my rock bottoms with. The people in my life before I change. Maybe my gut instinct isn't broken after all."

Trust Myself, Trust the Universe

Zak and I met at Gov's. He hated Dillon for hurting me and wanted to move back home. It felt fast and I worried that what had happened meant we were never as connected or happy as we should've been.

Needing a minute alone, I splashed cool water from the bathroom faucet onto my face. Looking in the mirror, I thought, *I wish I had my journals from before Alex killed himself.* I wanted written proof of what Zak and I were. What I was. When too much time passed, I wiped the water and walked back out toward Zak, only to be stopped by my friend's mom. "Amy! Hi! You remember who this is, right?"

Looking at the man next to her for a second, I recognized him to be my middle school principal. "Of course!"

"He remembers you!" She laughed.

"What?! Why?"

"You were always in the office!"

"I was? I don't remember that!"

"I shouldn't have said it."

"It's okay! Why was I?"

"I don't want to say!"

"What! Why!"

"I don't want to say." She smiled, shifting in her chair, avoiding my eyes.

Before Zak and I parted ways that night, I was still unable to say if he could move back home. "I'm sorry. I just think something's really wrong with my memory," I said.

Back at the house, I cried till it ran its course, then took my place on the porch, smoking and collecting the courage to call Lucas. "Were Zak and I happy in the beginning?" I asked.

"I think you guys were," was all he offered.

• • •

Leaning on my parents' kitchen counter, I told my mom, "It was so weird, I ran into Mont's mom at Gov's and she was like, 'You were always in the office,' but wouldn't say why. Do you remember that?"

"No!"

"What about the time Jamie said I went to therapy for being a liar. Was that around middle school?"

"That never happened!"

"Oh." I laughed and added, "Well, I don't trust my memory, so you have to pick if I try again with Zak!"

"Just try."

"Really?!"

"Yeah, if it doesn't work this time, at least you won't have regrets."

She assumed once more meant we'd test what we learned—him proving to be present. Me, honest.

Part of me was petrified though. Understanding I couldn't protect people with lies was different than putting it into practice.

I worried if I wasn't happy, I'd stay anyway.

• • •

The high school girls and I were in an ongoing group chat. Randomly, through regular reminiscing, they started to confirm things I thought were true but still questioned. Big things, like fights. Small things, like, "Did I score that goal from half field?

Oh yeah, I did." Tiny blocks to build my confidence.

Then there were the letters.

"I think you wrote it right before you moved away," Lucy said, sending me pictures of the front and back of a single sheet of paper. A handwritten request to ask her aunt, the school nurse, for information on how someone could get out of Hudson and away from drugs. Something I said I needed after Sam and I sat on the train tracks at 4 a.m., on a cocaine comedown. "I don't know what stopped us. Probably because no trains came," I read with no recollection of writing it.

My mother's sheets of paper came with no warning. "I found these in a box under my bed," she said, handing me a few loose pages, held together by the crease. The words folded inside were not visible to me yet. Along with it was a small, yellow legal pad too. My handwriting looked bubblier, younger.

Away from people, I read the yellow ones, still bound to the top.

"Mom + Dad,"

A suicide note.

Then one to Jamie too, ending with, "I loved you more than anyone else in the world…Please don't let anyone read my journal."

Flipping through to the end, I hoped for more words from young me, but found only blank pages.

The unfolded letter turned out to be typed. A formal explanation of why I needed to move away, for the second time, to be with Sam,

"I'm not just a little 16 year old that wants to run away," I said.

Like the texts from my friends, reading my letters solidified my story. They also made me imagine Heather's daughters saying any of that.

Or moving away.

They seemed so young.

Like babies.

They are, I thought.

I was, I thought, reshaping my memories.

No matter how mature my life had made me think I was, I was just a kid.

A kid writing that I wanted to die.

With no one to truly hear me.

· · ·

"We went to dinner at Rick's the other night," my mom said.

"What?! You guys ate at someone's house?!"

"He invited us for tacos!"

"You never do that!"

"I know, it was us and another couple."

"WHAT?! I can't believe you guys went."

"Rick started asking me about God!"

"I knew it! They were trying to recruit you to their church!"

"He kept asking me about God and I told him it wasn't something I thought about. I just don't think about it. And he kept asking, 'Don't you want to be with your daughters and John.' I told him I don't believe in that. When your body stops working, you die. That's it, you die. That's what I think."

"What did Dad say?"

"He didn't say anything, but get this—when we were driving home, I said, 'You didn't say anything about not believing in God.' And he said, 'I do believe in God. I prayed when Amy got lost at a concert that she'd be okay.'"

"What! How does he know that? Did I call him?"

"I don't know! I'm a bad mom! I was probably drunk on the couch," she laughed.

My dad came in from the garage.

"John, did Amy call you the night she was lost at the concert?"

"No, Sam did," he said and went into the kitchen.

"Wow. I can't believe that," I said.

"What?" my mom asked.

"I always question my memory, but it keeps being right."
"Really?"
"Yeah. Not to be a jerk, but I thought because you guys said stuff happened differently than I remembered, I was wrong."
"What stuff?"
"Like hitting."
"I remember the egg time," my mom said.

. . .

The egg time happened near Halloween. I was with my friend Clayton. Clayton died during motocross when I was around eleven or twelve. The egg time happened near then.

Clayton's mom and my mom thought it would be funny for me to throw eggs at a house down the street from us. The woman who lived in the house worked with my mom and Clayton's mom; they were all friends. My dad, not around while we hatched the plan, found the eggs missing from the fridge and beat me for it before I even left the house.

But, more than the incident itself, the egg time reminded me of the day I chose to fully forgive my parents.

I was eighteen. Sam and I sat on the back of my parents' boat. The mood was light. Maybe we were talking about something dumb I had done as a kid. Without wanting an apology, casually in the conversation, I brought up being hit.

"We didn't hit you," my parents said.

"Well, they did. But only when you deserved it," Jamie laughed.

"Not the egg time," I laughed too, instead of sharing what I really thought.

The time before middle school when the Walmart security guard chased Hopper and me out onto the hot pavement. Halfway through the parking lot, we turned back. Hopper's mom stood in front of the sliding doors yelling, "What are you guys doing?!" Inside, we were brought to the back of the building where I sat in a folding chair made of metal. It stung the bare back of my legs as I tried my hardest not to smile. Mostly though, I remembered the man photographing one torn open Life Savers roll—proof that I had stolen the three missing candies. Then my mom was there, walking me out through an aisle full of cookies and crackers, hitting me. Hard. In the head. Enough times that strangers stared, and Hopper's mom whispered, "Stop, Patti."

I thought of the time too, not long after Walmart, when Hopper and I left during the day. "Going for a walk," we yelled. When the summer sun set, we ran home in the rain. We laughed at how stupid we were, "Why are we running now, it won't help us?" It was too late to be saved by a few minutes' shed. My mom agreed. Hopper's mom said, "Stop Patti," that time too.

Then there were the times with my dad, mostly my *talking back* that bothered him. I was a child who endlessly asked, "Why?" and could never be satisfied with, "Because I said so." But there were other, more concrete crimes too—around the ninth grade when I argued with a police officer who had no evidence that the six pack and bag of weed he found was mine. "You didn't see me throw it onto the lawn," I said. Once at the station though, my tone changed and I pleaded, "Please don't call my dad." After being hit there, I swore that the look in the officer's eye said, "Sorry kid, maybe we shouldn't have called him."

Even the egg time, had my dad not stopped me, I would have thrown them. This was why, to an extent, I agreed with what Jamie said, I deserved it. I was the bad one, and I knew none of it was ever done out of malice. I knew each time I was hit, it followed something I had done. It was a response to me. A way to protect me, to shape me into a well-behaved human. They were simply using the methods modeled to them by their parents, something I couldn't fault them for. Plus, taking the blame away from them made more sense in the rest of our story –

They loved me.

I knew that. I never questioned it.

After the boat, on the way back home to Pennsylvania, Sam asked if I was okay. I was, I told him, because I had already silently decided I would never bring it back up. It didn't matter; I truly believed that. Then and forever after.

But my mother's acknowledgment of the egg time along with the confirmations of my high school friends gave me a gift I didn't know could be had:

Confidence to believe my own story.

No longer was I a person questioning, "Did that really happen?"

・ ・ ・

The shift from being so uncertain about my past to trusting it unlocked insights for me.

I realized when I told Nate that night in the bar, "No one is all bad, or all good. Everyone is trying their best," it was because I offered this excuse to my parents, and after them, I gave it easily to everyone else too, accidentally ingraining in me to love people despite being hurt by them.

Alexander was right when he mocked my saying, "He's a good singer!" and said, "You always see the good in everyone, even when they don't deserve it."

Love and pain could be one and the same for me.

・ ・ ・

On a hike, I wondered what else came from things I thought were no big deal. What would happen, I thought, if instead of saying to myself, "Other kids had it worse," I opened myself up to my actual experience, and trusted those too.

My mind drifted to the tenth grade. Shay pushed me from behind. "I'm not fighting on the first day of school," I said. The second day, she did it again, spitting "Pussy bitch" along with other spiteful words. The third day of school, Shay said some of the same things and shoved me again. The difference that day though, was she pulled my hair as I walked away. Without a word, I took my blue bag off my back and placed it gently on the hallway floor. A blur. Then Shay and I were in the office. The bone near her eye was bleeding badly. In the hallway, kids congratulated me, "You beat the shit out of her, Ame!"

That was not a new memory, but the repressed part that came after was—me, alone in my bedroom, after the fight in school. Writing, "I'm never having kids."

Mile marker three, I understood why I wasn't mad when Sam left me places or ripped Bunny's ear off; why I didn't get mad when Nate tried to trade me for drugs and stole my money. I got sad because being afraid to hit another person made me subconsciously suffocate my anger, in an attempt to control it.

. . .

Understanding why I banned anger begged me to look at why I then tied guilt to my only coping emotion. Unable to find its origins, writing did enable me to witness when it fully formed, after Aunt Karen.

"Not my mother. No right to be sad" bled into every other loss. Like skipping the funeral for my friend because "Other people were closer to him than me. I had no right to go." Or the countless times I told myself, *Not my father...not my husband... not my brother...no right to be sad.*

Its reach stretched further than the death of other people; it affected how I mourned the loss of myself too—the toy box, the Skate Factory, being called a slut and countless other times of unwanted sexual experiences forced me into a world where I was no longer a girl unnoticed, where boys didn't want to climb trees, build forts, and be friends. They wanted more. Being abruptly stripped from the adventurous, curious creature I was, with no capacity to know or name what I grieved for, I carved those tiny slits into my little wrist and let guilt flow through them. *Be happy people think you're pretty. At least you aren't bullied. You have no right to be sad.*

Genuinely unable to understand any of it at that age, over and over again I asked myself, *What is wrong with you? Why can't you just be happy?* It made sense that I swallowed what alcohol had to offer.

Solutions.

First a mask, "You're more fun when you drink." Then after, a tangible thing to fix. A mantra—*fix my drinking, fix myself*—because the correlation was clear: alcohol allowed me to let my guard down. Letting it down allowed people authorization in. A kiss, a drug dripped into my drink. This poured the guilt on thicker. I had no right to feel sad because I couldn't see situations as bad, only my actions in them. Me, as bad.

With each mistake, each failure to control my intake of everything, I hurt my own heart and hated myself more and more, completing the endless loop of practicing gratitude in the ugliest way: *You have no right to want to die. It's your fault you're sad. Other people have it worse than you.*

• • •

Less than a total of ten times seeing the therapist, he said, "I don't know what else I can say to you."

We both thought because I didn't want to kill myself, because I handled my heartbreak so well, I was done. Months later though, while the dust still settled from the Dillon situation, I remembered it was never about him; the therapist and I lost sight of the final line in our first email exchange, "I don't want to keep making the same mistakes in my life that I did since I was a teenager." Since I was a teenager.

Re-reading the typed letter to my parents, the clue to what lingered and tormented my core was hidden so clearly that it popped off the page, "Sam can't trust me to stay, and I don't blame him."

Part of why I left was because I hated who I was. Hated what I did to Sam. Before him too, I strayed and tried to stay with sweet but verbally abusive Bobby too. This, I thought, was why no matter what I did—moved, found jobs and apartments, put myself through college, became a counselor and caseworker, an adult—I felt like an imposter. I never healed from what I hated most.

Being a cheater.

Knowing it was about connection, never sex, I still had to answer why I didn't know how to leave Bobby. Sam. Zak. Anyone.

Peeling away the layers I lived behind, my answer came clearly.

Death.

Death drilled into me the desperation to know, "What is the point?"

This trauma didn't care when I told myself, *You have no right to ask that. To feel that.* It demanded an answer. Love became my response. Boys, the technique. They replaced bonds needed.

From the deceased.

From my family.

From culture and community.

From religion.

Leaving by choice would have been the ultimate betrayal to myself, an incomprehensible sacrifice to my survival.

This too was why I assigned meaning when they ended. Sam, my savior. Nate, my suicide rock bottom. Dillon, my muse. That made my soul say:

We mattered.

Love mattered.

LIFE mattered.

∙ ∙ ∙

Lando at my side, I looked out toward the Hudson River. Clouds clutched the crisp Catskill Mountains, my continuous love. Listening to the sound of the ice cracking, I breathed in the air and felt it:

Boys were no longer my fix.

I knew it too, when mid-May brought bright-green grass, lush moss, and the sweet smell of honeysuckle. And again, walking through the field full of wildflowers, shutting my eyes for a few paces, letting Lando guide me as I listened to birds chirping and the sun soaked and seeped into me. A slight breeze brushed my hair across my face, and I said to myself, *THIS IS THE POINT.*

∙ ∙ ∙

My journey to change behaviors I'd had since I was a teenager brought me to a place of being able to trust not only my memories but my inner voice in the moment. This made me comfortable with being still. Being more peaceful inside allowed me the ability to look out and feel it too. I marveled at how magical it was to live on a planet where food literally grew from the ground and almost nine million species of animals roamed around. Finally, I was free from the girl who stood in front of Faith Christian Academy and declared, "Fuck you, God." Free from the woman questioning if nature was enough too; I knew it was.

Undiagnosed

Walking the blue trail, I had a persistent feeling: *Call Mom.* Not being the type to talk on the phone with people, my parents included, I listened to the feeling.

"Yellow," I said.

"Whatcha doing, Ame?

"Nothing. Just got back from a dog walk."

"Oh."

"What's wrong?" I asked.

"I'm just tired."

"Did something happen?"

She explained family drama—Sara and a birthday party mishap that made us uninvited because of Aunt Lia. Then her best friend Carol called to say in a gossipy way, "I heard Ralph overdosed again. They're keeping him in the hospital this time because he aspirated." To which my mom responded, "What the fuck, Carol, are you telling me my nephew died?"

"What does that mean, aspirated?" I asked my mom.

"That's what killed Janis Joplin and Jimi Hendrix."

"Is Ralph okay?"

"I don't want to bother Aunt Marie."

"Maybe message her on Facebook or something so she knows you're thinking about her but doesn't have to talk if she doesn't want to."

"Yeah, maybe I'll do that."

"You just sound sad," I said.

"I'm just done with people."

"Not me!"

"No, you made me feel better already."

Back home, I pumped a dollop of face wash into my hand and thought how much I'd miss my mother, who gave me the floral-scented scrub. I hoped I was here to make her happier; to be there for her as she had been for me. *Without her I'd have no clothes. No bra for sure,* I thought, knowing shopping wasn't something I did for fun with friends. It wasn't even a thing I particularly liked in general, but tolerated while with my mom, and Jamie too. Even with them though, I never purchased a bra.

Instead, every year for Christmas, Jamie and I unwrapped at least two, until my mom finally believed me when I told her she was spending too much money on us and stopped putting them under the tree. But even after that, because my mom was the type to give me hand-me-downs with price tags still on them, I got three more, which I've been wearing since. For six years.

My mind still with my mother, I sifted through the hundreds of mini nail files she gave me. All decorated differently: purple llamas with sombreros, pink flamingos, and flowers too. Choosing and using one, my thoughts drifted, remembering random times.

My mom, standing in her underwear, stirring the huge pot of homemade meatballs on the stove after she insisted on giving me her Army-green pants, just because I said I liked them; then there were the plants she sent me home with too. Variations of spiders, devil's ivy, and cacti. My house would be empty without them, I thought before remembering a handful came from Zak's mom too.

"If we separated again, we'd have to each take our plants," I said in my head before slowly, unintentionally dividing our things.

He'd get the piano and Japanese artwork above it, passed down from generations in his family. Most of the furniture I bought, but I'd give him what he needed. The bed at least. The animals would have to stay again, they hadn't known any other home. *I'd offer him the house this time,* I thought before realizing he wouldn't want it. *I'd give him money from my savings,* I thought, planning a way for him to afford his own apartment; to not worry about money. Again, drafting a future for him so that he could go back to being a chef because being a car salesman, to make us fit, made him miserable. All I wanted was for him to be happy.

And me too.

Except, as much as I tried and acknowledged what I needed, I felt fucked anyway because my broken heart was taking too long to heal. The lingering feelings felt out of my control. I couldn't help that I remembered each article of clothing I wore with Dillon or that it made me miss him. The tank top from the black-and-white pictures, where he captured how I felt about him; the cotton crop top the night I got my hair cut and he said he'd have whatever I was having at the bar; the LL Bean blue flannel I wore to his sister's farm, when he put his flannel over mine for added warmth; the Army-style jacket I wore the first time I met his girls and the torn boyfriend-cut jeans that Dillon photographed me in when we ate mushrooms. Later, when he sent me the picture he had taken, he said, "I love you in those jeans." I remembered him when I passed restaurants we dined in and roads we traveled on too. Mostly though, each time I saw a white truck, my heart sank and I wished I could leave the state because the fleeting, unintentional dreams of him made me worry I had fallen back into old patterns, that my thoughts alone counted as unfaithful. For answers, on what it all meant and to make sure I wasn't ignoring my inner voice, I put the nail file from my mom back and fetched a pencil instead.

I journaled, *"Do I only think of Dillon because I'm healing from him? Does it matter at all he enters my thoughts as often as he does? Everything reminds me of him...It doesn't have to mean more than that. And I can't go back to him anyway, so* what does it matter? It doesn't.

But...Do I need to tell Zak about it? Or can I get over it on my own? Zak and I have both been so much better at communicating...but telling him I still think of Dillon would crush him. It would crush him even more if I said I mostly miss Dillon because Dillon had such a positive attitude, especially since I'm partially to blame for Zak's negative one. He is healing from what I did. From me. Maybe Dillon doesn't mean what I think he does, maybe he wasn't my muse. Maybe I simply need to give Zak time to get better from it all too.

The real problem is, I still want to find solutions before I say a word about anything because being quiet ensures that only I get hurt.

Except I already learned—THAT IS NOT TRUE.

Not so black and white though. I need to find where the line crosses between thinking and telling, for me.

Maybe the weekend away will help us. Then I'll figure it out."

When we fought some over sex he wanted when I wasn't ready and a dinner that he didn't have money for, I found later dates to let me decide. *Maybe once we open the restaurant, it will be better. If not, then I'll figure it out*, I told myself.

· · ·

MEMORIAL DAY WEEKEND 2020.
During the beginning of the pandemic, but prior to the peaceful protests and riots for George Floyd, I brought turkey subs over to my parents' pool. Jamie and her boyfriend sat with my parents and me on the porch. "I'm not wearing a mask in public," my dad said between bites, gently demanding his daughters to detect the importance of free choice. The topic drifted into helicopter parenting and my dad shared his philosophy on that too, "Let kids figure it out on their own."

Privately, Jamie and I joked they could have given us a little more guidance, especially when we dated terrible people.

Two days later, the temperature dropped twenty degrees. I wore a long-sleeve shirt, shorts, and hiking boots. Climbing through the mountain trails, I reflected on how fortunate I felt for having my mom and dad. For them letting me learn alone.

Had they brought me to some sort of talk therapy when I was young, maybe my verbal and internal communication would have become better sooner, but who would I be then.

Would I have fallen for journaling? The backbone of facing my mistakes, my mortality, of living a life examined.

Without writing, perhaps memoirs would not have become my mentors, podcasts and people's stories my saviors, gently guiding me toward core values of empathy and kindness, which I now offered to myself too.

With these parallel parents, I also imagined psychiatrists clinically calling me depressed and anxious, maybe naming me with borderline personality disorder too. In that universe, pills could have provided a darker plight; stuff sniffed, side effects unknown. A medicated Band-Aid may have also masked my self-diagnosed serotonin deficiency. My search for a solution for this could have been hindered too—the dots of school sports and motion as a conductor of dopamine never connected. Without that natural motivator, I wouldn't have wanted more of what made my mood better, me better: movement. Lifelong practices of consistently completing things like Tae Bo with Billy Blanks, P90X, and Insanity offered outlying returns too.

My body taught my mind what type of person I was.

I showed up to do the work, even when I didn't want to.

When it was hard, I fought to finish.

I never quit.

In my thirties, I could see how this subconscious mindset, built by my body but rooted with sentiments from my parents, followed me into life—each time I chose to be alive.

Into my art too. Each sentence, paragraph, and chapter where

I wouldn't stop, no matter how difficult it became because I had already proved that was who I was. Perhaps my parents had known it all along—that I was the type of kid who'd figure it out. "Figure it out," I said out loud, alone in the woods, because for the millionth time, reflections on the trail led to revelations.

Growing up this way was why the idea of practicing radical honesty could never work for me. Not being able to tell every thought in my head didn't mean I was being dishonest. Finding my own way over Dillon was okay; being aware of the guilt I felt for those thoughts was enough. I could acknowledge my feelings and move forward, with patience.

Replacing the pressure I created to share every thought with Zak with permission to think things through, alone, allowed me to put into practice what I learned through writing: nothing is wrong with me.

I question everything.

Myself.

Relationships.

Why to be alive.

I am a thinker.

A seeker for finding my truth.

I thank my parents for letting me do it this way, trampling through the world. Alone.

A Love Letter

On the sixth floor, I looked out the glass-wall windows to the path along the water far below me. I watched joggers with dogs of every size and fluffiness, women pushing expensive strollers wearing workout gear that cost more than most things I owned, and ferries crossing the Hudson River from the Hoboken side to New York City, delivering people to their places, as Jamie jokingly said, "Look, a boat," mocking my mom, in the most endearing way.

"Should we go sit in the sun and drink beers?" I asked.

"Where?" Jamie said.

"It doesn't look like there's people at the pier yet, we could go there before it gets crowded?"

"Okay!"

"I'll shower first," I said.

Choosing the tall, red bottle of shampoo, I squeezed just enough to let the scent of sweet orchid lily seep out. Her shaving cream, called Summertime, smelled heavenly too; I thought about how her things were always richer than mine.

Stepping out onto the plush bathmat, the room stayed steamy, with no window or vent, while I perused the items in the medicine cabinet, picking a moisturizer I'd never used. In Jamie's bedroom, I chose a lotion from the basket that sat on her dresser. Besides my underwear, I dressed in all her clothes, rituals I'd done every time I was in her home. Spritzing a tiny bit of Coco Mademoiselle, I thought, *I'd miss this.* The smell and feel of all her conditioners, creams, and perfumes.

Jamie.

I imagined a life where I wasn't here, where I didn't allow her and my parents to become my placeholders, my reasons to stay alive when I couldn't find my own.

I would have missed so much.

Our sister trips. Our concerts in the rain because bad weather followed Jamie: hurricanes in Florida, mudslides in Big Sur, wildfires in Portland, a cyclone in Iceland, and even a seaweed storm when we went to Tulum.

I thought of how much I would have missed meeting Jamie at the halfway point between my house and hers, for a hike.

"Zak thought we were hiking the whole Adirondack Trail! He made me bring a compass, a knife, and this bracelet that turns into a rope, a whistle, and can be used to make a fire!"

"Wanna see what I brought?" Jamie asked.

"What?!"

"FACEMASKS!"

"How would we even wash that off after?" I asked, laughing.

"I brought these too!" Jamie said, showing me pink grapefruit Neutrogena face wipes.

Not at the peak, but a cool spot close to the top, we ate pink lady apples I brought. Throwing the core into the woods, Jamie made a joke about an applelanche, "Like an avalanche, but with apples."

I'd miss that too, laughing with Jamie, which was different than laughing with anyone else.

More than all of that though, I would have missed being there for Jamie during her dark times, which we both agreed was when we really became close, when she no longer pretended to be perfect, to be a good example to me.

. . .

Back in New York, I felt it too.

After swimming in my parents' pool when I'd ask my mom, "Braid my hair?"

Then again, as the air blew through the massive, metal fan inside my dad's semi–newly built three bay garage while he showed me his progress—the final coat of black paint on the '75 corvette along with windows that were installed in the Firebird, my favorite, from 1967 and the color of solid, silky emeralds.

The feeling was there too when we went for boat rides as a family and then again when I was alone in the Jeep with no top or doors on; just me, the wind, and the night sky.

• • •

I thought about it more as I walked across the street from my house to the conservation park and traveled on the same forested earth where I found myself. *I would have missed the trails. The walks in the rain. The hot showers afterward.*

In my yard it happened while I watched my black cat roll around in grass the exact color of his eyes and thought, *I would have missed Chester if I killed myself.*

Chester Bear was almost not ours. At the rescue, there were three floors of unwanted cats and I picked a little orange guy napping in the sun, but Zak said, "No, let's get this one," because he liked how it kept meowing, until we had him home. Then it was no longer cute, we were being woken up before alarm clocks by Chester's meows. Every day. For a decade.

But, even with that, we knew Chester was the best choice. He came when he was called. He followed us inside and out. He ate Doritos, drank out of mud puddles, and sunbathed in herb boxes too narrow for him to fit in. He rolled around in dirt and after I cleaned cobwebs and dried lawn clippings from his head, he'd saunter inside to find the perfect bed.

Every time I found Chester in a drawer left open and

unattended, his rolls overflowing; in a basket full of folded clean clothes; on our pillows for the morning sun; the bed in the guest room for the afternoon or the back of the couch to catch the last sliver before it set behind the Catskills, I thought about how happy I was to witness his great comfortable finds, to watch his fat belly move with each soft breath as he slept in such peace.

The sun carried me back to memories of Broadus that never faded, and I knew I would have missed those too.

At the boat, Bro's nose, brown, full of dirt from a day of pushing rocks into the river as he retired onto the gray wooden dock, dozing the daylight hours away.

In Fort Lauderdale, running with me as I rollerbladed to the Big Dog on Wednesdays so Jack the bartender could feed him too many hot dogs.

Our walks, everywhere.

Really the ones after work with our Swedish people in Hudson though. And after. When we parted ways from them and headed to the Red Dot for late-night fires in the pit on the patio so that I could feel in flow, lost in time and connected through conversations with strangers.

• • •

Had I killed myself, Hawaii, my heaven, would have never happened either. Neither would the day trip to Alabama Jack's in Key Largo, where I drank beer from a can till the Grateful Dead cover band ended. There would have been none of the restaurants: Applebee's and "Apple-buddies" in Pennsylvania, Primanti Brothers with Jen and Jimmy Jam in Florida, 168 in New York. The places where cooks and waitstaff became family, especially when I didn't have my own there.

• • •

I would have missed the boys who gave me space to be safe in certain ways. Sam, Jake, Ben, the Head Chef, and my husband, who just placed a full French press on a striped cloth napkin next to the bed. Along with it, my tin coffee cup with what looks like watercolor painted trees too—so I could write these last chapters. He offers this support, this love, knowing what my book is about.

. . .

The book.

I would have missed the book and its ability to continually challenge me during the dark moments of the night, where by force or choice, I created loneliness and craved more out of life. It challenged me too when a slew of good days ended and the old me slithered in, waking up feeling off for no apparent reason, or worse for a reason. For thoughts I wished weren't there or feelings like I failed because of conversations or actions that happened the night before, the book was there, confronting me. *Have you changed enough? Who are you to write?*

But equally so when I listened to the soft pull calling from within to enjoy the sound of the rain that rushed down. To sift through Spotify and settle into the sound of Sonata No. 42, the book answered me too.

As I put my practices on the page, the book showed me where my authority to write came from. It was from my pursuit, not my perfection. The proof of progress had been in my recovery time, which was now quick because of habits that mended me.

When I woke up feeling off, I immediately stepped into my yard and stretched on the stones that led to the fire pit because I knew outside fixed me instantly. That fresh air allowed me the energy to put a harness on the pup and walk into the woods to start the process of forgiving and loving myself all over. When unwanted thoughts lingered longer, I baked something to distract myself. I made coffee and a smoothie to be mindful. I thanked the people who farmed the beans, the blueberries, the bananas, everything in it, graciously given to me from the Earth. I remained conscious to not only ingest movement and food that was good for me but information too—reading books or listening to podcasts to gain insight, clarity, and curiosity. I kept with my gratitude and knew I was lucky for so many reasons. When none of those things worked though, I sat with the gift the book gave me, a twisted core of optimism that I wouldn't always feel that way and certainty that even if I did, I'd be okay.

I'd figure it out.

Mostly, I would have missed how the book fought the meaninglessness for me. It filled my spare time with purpose, with intentions so clear that finally, I could answer the question I had asked all along: *What is the point?*

The Road to Hell Is Paved with Good Intentions

At Hudson Valley Community College, surrounding the Nate times, I was unable to concentrate on RNA and the molecular level of life because I was in fight or flight and functioning at the bottom levels of Maslow's pyramid. With a brain in the thick of pain and unable to see beyond tears, my ability to marvel, to be in awe, was gone; I was blind to the magic of it all.

Life.

Nature.

Being.

My being caught in that mindset for over a decade, and coming out of it, drove this book. I wanted to tell those versions of me, who felt like life could never be different.

It is.

It changed.

. . .

Understanding my message was what gave me the strength to push past my biggest fear, that my truth would ultimately hurt the people I loved most—my family, Zak and his family, Alexander's family too—but I had to go back in time through them, because as much as I felt alone, I was not. I hope my words never bring pain and that the intention of the story is clear, there is hope.

Hold on.

. . .

"Your life is your life
Don't let it be clubbed into dank submission
Be on the watch.
There are ways out.
There is a light somewhere.
It may not be much light but
It beats the darkness."

Charles Bukowski

Afterword

SOMETIME IN 2022
After the earlier chapters of this book were written, Nate sent me a message explaining that his previous partner had blocked my number without him knowing, which was why he stopped communicating with me. After that, we picked up random check-ins with each other.

JUNE 7, 2022
Nate sent me a video clip from *Anchorman*. "This always reminds me of you!"

We made jokes back and forth about the movie before I asked, "How's Atlanta?"

"It's amazing. The people here are so nice! It's like a bunch of Amys everywhere you go! Also, no snow! Also, I got a dog!" Seconds later, three pictures of an adorable black lab came through.

"What's his name?"

"Dogg! He's named after Broadus's alter ego!"

"Awwww I love that and that you got a dog!"

"I thought you would appreciate it!"

THE NEXT DAY NATE wrote, "Hey not to be a weirdo, but can you send me a picture of your tattoo/sleeve? I want to show Kate."

I sent one.

He sent a picture back. His elbow to shoulder, full of colorful ink. "Finally got the space tat I wanted!"

"Oh cool! Yeah, that's been a long time in the making," I said.

"This is my newest one," he said and sent a picture of the Pink Panther with a thought bubble above his head that read "God isn't real."

"This is my newest one!" I said, sending a photo of my lower bicep with the words "GODS & WORMS" written in a courier, typewriter font. "So strange we both chose God but not God tattoos for our last ones!"

"Great minds!" he wrote.

November 24, 2022
I sent, "Happy Thanksgiving! Remember that Thanksgiving Broadus pooped turkey allll over your carpet. Bro Bro classic. I hope you are so happy!!!"

March 16, 2023
At Upper Depot Brewing Co., my husband drank Staley's IPA out of mug 44, I drank the same but out of number 27. As we finished looking through his camera roll, to pick a picture for the announcement of the soft opening of his food truck in two days, a small group of people entered the bar. One woman, who I knew through Kaia and Phil, came over and started to say hello as a man squeezed through and said, "Can I interrupt? Hi Amy!"

It took me a few seconds to remember who it was.

Nate's stepfather.

I had bumped into him a few times over the years and I was always glad that I had.

"Hi," I said.

"Hey, Amy!" he said in an upbeat tone before asking, "Have you heard about Nate?"

Immediately I thought, *he's dead*. But I said, "No."

As the stepfather looked down and scrolled through his phone, I thought that maybe he was going to show me that Nate had another baby or won some type of award, but because so much time passed, I eventually, half-jokingly, blurted out, "He didn't die, right?"

"He did, I'm looking for his obituary."

His tone still seemed upbeat.

It didn't match the words he was saying.

Especially "suicide."

Tears came fast and unexpectedly as I said, "But he told me he was so happy in Atlanta."

"He was. He had a really nice girlfriend. They bought a house together. He'd been sober for eight or ten years."

He started to say more about Nate doing drugs at the end. I didn't know if he meant that Nate killed himself because he relapsed or that Nate purposely purchased drugs to die that day, like he and I had tried many years ago.

I didn't ask anything. I couldn't. But Nate's stepfather kept talking.

The last thing I caught was that it happened in August.

"Oh, that's why he didn't respond when I messaged him on Thanksgiving."

I stopped looking at the stepfather and faced forward, toward the bartender. "Do you have a cigarette?" I asked.

She didn't. She gave me lavender oil to smell and crystals to hold.

I heard Nate's stepfather say to my husband, "Sorry to leave her like this."

I was grateful my husband and I had driven separately to the Upper Depot. Alone in my Jeep, the heavy cries that I held back in front of other people came out. The same thought repeated over and over again in my mind.

I wish he called.

I wish he called.

I wish he called.

Then my brain drifted to this book, which made me feel selfish and psychotic. But I wanted Nate to be here. I wanted him to be here in case the book did what we wanted, helped people. I wanted him to be proud of himself, and proud of me. I wanted him to see that our pain mattered; our love mattered; our story mattered; we mattered. Then, briefly, I wondered if maybe none of it did, since he ended up dead anyway.

The next morning, when I felt slightly stronger, I found his obituary online. Whoever wrote it described how Nate would do anything he could to help anyone, anytime; that Nate believed that no matter how low a person got, they deserved a fresh pair of socks, and so Nate routinely bought all the socks in a store and delivered them to the unhoused community. It was not lost on me that the last time I saw Nate, he offered me his own socks, because my feet were cold and I couldn't find mine.

After the obituary, I read through the comments and found comfort in the stories shared. From people in recovery saying that Nate was the first friend to so many. From his daughter, who spoke of lessons of giving and generosity learned. It reminded me of the beauty of kindness; of Nate; of how much it all mattered, even though none of it was everlasting.

· · ·

Mexican culture has a concept known as the three deaths. The first death is understanding your own mortality; learning that you will die; that you are a conscious creature who contemplates the meaning of life; of existence (GODS). The second death happens when your physical body, your organs—your brain and heart—stop working; when you cease to exist (WORMS). The third death is the last time your name is ever spoken. For most of us, this will happen in just a few generations.

Maybe this third death is what subconsciously drove me to

write this. To keep Nate (Alexander, Joey, and Aunt Karen) alive, as long as I could. Maybe it also made me write the chapter "Love Letter" for my family; to prepare for what I know will inevitably happen. In the beginning though, my intention had nothing to do with that. It was always about fostering self-forgiveness and saying: You do not have to die for your perceived mistakes, not relapsing, not cheating, nothing; you are not bad or broken; the feeling of hopelessness is a lie, a trick; you do not have to suffer silently; CALL.

GET HELP

- Suicide and Crisis Lifeline: 988
- National Suicide Prevention Lifeline: 1-800-273-8255
- National Domestic Violence Hotline: 1-800-799-7233
- SAMHSA's National Helpline (Mental and/or substance use disorders: 1-800-662-4357
- Local Department of Social Services—look up your county. They can help connect you to services, such as local domestic violence shelters, mental health clinics, and substance abuse programs. They can also help if you are homeless or need emergency assistance and food.

Fin,
With LOVE.

Thank You

This book would not have been possible without the support from the following people: Elisabeth A., Jesse C., Courtney M., Todd B., Steve B., Zoey A., Marielle Y., Chesley M., Anna R., Matt S., Jodie MR., Ang R., Lea K., Squeak K., Andy A., Danielle Sk., Tanicia O., Katie H., Amanda S., Lindsey RG, Sarah G., Jake C., Mikey N., Ari, Desiree S., Wendy R., Theresa S., Jen W., Elaine K., Courtney T., Willy C., Rudy M., Colleen., Mike C., Lynn G., Katrina K., Jen W., Meg E., Dee., Laurie Chittenden, Vanessa Mendozzi, and Brooks Becker.

Biggest thank you to my brother, sister, father, and husband—I love you.

Rip this page out and pass it along.

Get Help

- Suicide and Crisis Lifeline: 988
- National Suicide Prevention Lifeline: 1-800-273-8255
- National Domestic Violence Hotline: 1-800-799-7233
- SAMHSA's National Helpline (Mental and/or substance use disorders: 1-800-662-4357
- Local Department of Social Services—look up your county. They can help connect you to services, such as local domestic violence shelters, mental health clinics, and substance abuse programs. They can also help if you are homeless or need emergency assistance and food.

CPSIA information can be obtained
at www.ICGtesting.com
Printed in the USA
LVHW090905180723
752741LV00003B/392